120

Quick and Easy

OBJECT Lessons

for *Children's* STORY TIME

Jim Simmons

 **Pacific Press®**
Publishing Association
Nampa, Idaho | Oshawa, Ontario, Canada
www.pacificpress.com

Cover design by Gerald Lee Monks
Cover design resources from iStockphoto.com
Inside design by Kristin Hansen-Mellish

The author assumes full responsibility for the accuracy of all facts and quotations as cited in this book.

Scripture quotations marked KJV are from the King James Version.

Scripture quotations marked NABRE are taken from the New American Bible, revised edition © 2010, 1991, 1986, 1970 Confraternity of Christian Doctrine, Inc., Washington, DC. All Rights Reserved.

Scripture quotations marked NET are from the NET Bible®, copyright ©1996–2006 by Biblical Studies Press, LLC. http://netbible.com. All rights reserved.

Scripture quotations marked NIV are from the HOLY BIBLE, NEW INTERNATIONAL VERSION®. Copyright © 1973, 1978, 1984, 2011 by Biblica, Inc.® Used by permission. All rights reserved worldwide.

Scripture quotations marked NKJV are taken from the New King James Version®. Copyright © 1982 by Thomas Nelson. Used by permission. All rights reserved.

Scripture quotations marked NLT are taken from the Holy Bible, New Living Translation, copyright © 1996, 2004, 2007, 2013 by Tyndale House Foundation. Used by permission of Tyndale House Publishers, Inc., Carol Stream, Illinois 60188. All rights reserved.

Additional copies of this book are available by calling toll-free 1-800-765-6955 or by visiting http://www.AdventistBookCenter.com.

Library of Congress Cataloging-in-Publication Data
Names: Simmons, James, 1943- author. | Harris, Feryl, editor.
Title: 120 quick and easy object lessons for children's story time :
    illustrations for children's stories / James Simmons ; edited by Feryl Harris.
Other titles: One hundred twenty quick and easy object lessons for children's story time | One
    hundred and twenty quick and easy object lessons for children's story time
Description: Nampa : Pacific Press Publishing, 2016.
Identifiers: LCCN 2016000398 | ISBN 9780816361236 (pbk.)
Subjects: LCSH: Object-teaching. | Christian education of children. | Christian education—
    Teaching methods.
Classification: LCC BV1536.5 .S56 2016 | DDC 268/.432—dc23 LC record available at
    http://lccn.loc.gov/2016000398

March 2016

Dedication

I would like to dedicate this book to Feryl Harris, who was our downstairs neighbor in Hawaii for all the years we lived and worked there. Feryl was killed in an automobile accident two weeks after she completed the editing of my stories.

During the seven years we worked together at the Hawaii Conference of Seventh-day Adventists, Feryl encouraged me to locate my handwritten and typed notes from presentations I made prior to moving to Hawaii. She recommended I type them in a format that could be sent to publishers. She was aware that I shared my stories with local churches and leaders of children's departments as I traveled around the conference. She read several stories and had seen the children's responses to those I told at the churches.

Without her encouragement and editing talents, these stories would not be here to assist you in presenting real-life illustrations to your young children.

Contents

Introduction

The stories included in this book of object lessons for children are made up of many simple items that are readily available and are used in everyday life. God has blessed me with story ideas, which I have endeavored to match with various items, to illustrate the spiritual lessons of life in a way that children can understand. These are written as though I were telling the story to children; actual and possible replies to the questions asked were added to help the storyteller understand my replies and/or follow-up questions. Read a story ahead of time so that you can prepare the illustration items and know its theme, and then present it in your own words.

While I have attempted not to copy the stories of others, you may have previously heard similar details as I have shared my story outlines and told the stories in a variety of congregations both on the mainland and in Hawaii.

I pray you will be able to pass these illustrations on to the children of your church as they commit them to memory in their growing years. It has been my pleasure that many adults who heard these stories as children are now telling them to their congregations of young children.

The theme of each object lesson can be found here.

Each object lesson is numbered; a full list of titles can be found on the contents page in the front of the book.

Locks

"Ask and it will be given to you; seek and you will find; knock and the door will be opened to you."
—Matthew 7:7, NIV

What You Need:
➤ one key lock
➤ one combination lock
➤ one group of keys
➤ one list of numbers

➤ Here is the list of materials needed to illustrate the object lesson.

I have two things in my bag that serve the same purpose, but they are different. Do you need some clues? Sometimes they are open and sometimes not. Need more clues? Sometimes you need a key, but sometimes you need to know numbers. Sometimes they can keep things in, and sometimes they can keep things out. Now can you guess? *(Locks.)*

I have two kinds of locks. Is there a difference? What is it? One is a combination lock, and it is opened by turning the dial back and forth with specific numbers. Do you think it matters which way you turn the dial and what numbers you use? *(Yes.)* (I will tell you more about that in another story.) The other lock and is opened with a key. Does it matter which key we use? Yes. Because the correct key, the lock will still be locked.

As you grow older, you will have different keys. You'll probably need a house key, a locker key, a car key, and an office key at work.

There is a special key for everyone's needs. This key is spoken about in the Bible, and it will keep us in touch with Jesus. Can you guess what it is? *(Prayer!)* If we pray to Jesus every day, He will open the right doors so that we will do what He has planned for us. Keeping in touch with Him every day will keep us happy no matter what happens, because we know we can trust Him. He can help us choose good friends, good things to read, good games to play, good things to watch, good things to eat—all the choices we make every day.

You will learn that Jesus can and will help you in everything you do all day long because He is your friend. Raise your hand if you want Jesus to protect you by teaching you to use the key to His prayer lock of safety.

An Apple a Day

What You Need:
- one apple
- children's daily devotional books

"Do you not know that your bodies are temples of the Holy Spirit, who is in you, whom you have received from God? You are not your own."
—1 Corinthians 6:19, NIV

Have you boys and girls ever heard the saying "An apple a day keeps the doctor away"? *(Yes. No.)* Do you know why people say it? Apples are good for us because they are part of eating a well-balanced diet, which includes fruit, nuts, grains, vegetables, dairy products, and other good foods.

Have you ever seen someone take an apple to his or her teacher and give it as a gift? I don't know if children still do that, but when I was young, a long time ago, boys and girls would do that. Do you know why? Sometimes it was because they wanted their teachers to treat them special. But most of the time, they gave apples to their teachers because they wanted their teachers to know that they liked them and because they knew apples were healthy.

If apples help keep your body healthy, what other things can you do to keep yourself healthy? *(Go to bed on time, get a good night's sleep, exercise, and eat a good diet; those are a few, but there are more.)* What about staying healthy with God? Can eating an apple do that for you? *(This is a trick question.)* Yes, because it helps keep your body strong and healthy, which makes God happy. But what else do you need? *(Pray, study your Sabbath School lesson, read your Bible, love and obey your parents, love your brothers and sisters and, don't forget, your friends.)* These are all good things! I would like to suggest something else that will make you strong and healthy with God. Have your mother or father read to you or read for yourself a daily devotional book for children. Let me show you a few. They are full of good and interesting stories that will let you see just how good God is.

Just like an apple a day helps to keep you from getting sick, a little extra time in the morning with Jesus will help keep you on the happy road to heaven. Ask your mom and dad to take time to read and pray with you every day.

An Apple

"In the beginning God created
the heavens and the earth."
—Genesis 1:1, NIV

I have something in my bag that is sometimes yellow, sometimes green, and sometimes red. Can you guess what it is? (Let the children guess.) Need another clue? OK, it is round. Sometimes you can eat it and sometimes not. What I have is an apple.

Why do you think you sometimes shouldn't eat the apple? Maybe it isn't ripe yet. *(An unripe apple can give you a tummy ache.)* Maybe it has bruises in places and is spoiled. Maybe someone already started to eat it, and it has turned brown. Also, not all apples are tasty to eat fresh, but they are good when you bake them in a pie with cinnamon and sugar.

Do you know the correct way to cut an apple? *(Top to bottom?)* You could do that. But if you cut it around the middle, from side to side, God has something special for you to see. Would you like to see it? What shape does it remind you of? It looks like a five-pointed star! If you cut it from top to bottom, you will miss seeing that special star God placed in every apple.

God has given us many beautiful things to see. Can you name a few of those beautiful things? *(Sky, trees, mountains, oceans, flowers.)* What about our family and friends? Some of His special gifts are small, like the star shape in apples.

Every time you cut an apple, remember which way to cut it so that you can see God's present for you! Look for other hidden things God has made special for you to see. I am sure you will find other little presents from God.

Artificial Sweetener

"Kind words are like honey—sweet
to the soul and healthy for the body."
—Proverbs 16:24, NLT

What You Need:
➤ one packet of sugar
➤ one packet of Sweet'N Low

I have two things in my bag today. Both are used for the same thing, but one is real and the other is not real—it's artificial. Can you guess what they are? Need more clues? Both are sweet. *(Show them the sugar and Sweet'N Low.)*

Did you know that some boys and girls are like Sweet'N Low? Do you know why? They are artificially sweet. Do you know what I mean by "artificially sweet"? They are *sweet* (good) only when they want something. Many boys and girls are like real sugar. They are sweet all the time. Are any of you boys and girls like Sweet'N Low (artificially sweet)?

Did you know that sometimes Christians are *real* and sometimes *artificial*? A real Christian loves Jesus *every* day and wants to obey Jesus *all* the time. Artificial Christians will only do the right thing when they want something or when they are in Sabbath School or church. Sometimes they are good just to try to fool others.

I hope you will remember when you see sugar or Sweet'N Low that you want to *always* be sweet like real sugar and to be good because you always love Jesus.

What You Need:
▸ one hand-stitched picture with the back visible

The Right View

"But the LORD said to Samuel, 'Don't judge by his appearance or height, for I have rejected him. The LORD doesn't see things the way you see them. People judge by outward appearance, but the LORD looks at the heart.' "

—1 Samuel 16:7, NLT

I have a beautiful stitchery picture that a friend has made. Would you like to see it? (Show the children the back side.) Isn't that beautiful? No! Why not? *(There are loose strings.)* What a mess. I thought you would like the picture! It looks great to me! What I am looking at is beautiful. Oh, you want to see the part that I am looking at! OK. (Flip to the finished side.) Is the picture prettier now? *(Yes.)* What made the difference? (Looking at the finished side.)

Do you know that sometimes we look at other boys and girls who may not have nice clothes or toys or who don't talk the same as we or our friends talk? So, we decide we don't want to play with them because they are different from us.

Have you ever seen that happen? Sometimes we are looking at the wrong side or only the outside of that person. I am glad that Jesus looks past our clothes, our toys, our houses, and our cars and *only* sees what our hearts are like. He can see if our hearts are like this beautiful picture. Remember, we are all like pictures whether we are young or old. If we ask Jesus every day, He will help us to be like a beautiful picture. The more we are like Jesus, the prettier our pictures will be because Jesus is still helping us. He is coming soon to take His beautiful "pictures" home to heaven. I want all of us to be there together.

Your Protector —Balloon 1

What You Need:
- balloons of various shapes and colors
- one pin
- one shield

"After this, the word of the LORD came to Abram in a vision: 'Do not be afraid, Abram. I am your shield, your very great reward.' "
—Genesis 15:1, NIV

If you boys and girls are happy today, raise your hands high! Good. Does Jesus want you to be happy? Would you like to see what I have in my bag? When I see what is in here, it makes me think of happy boys and girls. It's a balloon. See how it flies so easily. Can you tell me someplace where you see balloons? (*Birthday parties, circus.*) Those are places where boys and girls are usually happy, smiling, and laughing.

So what happens when Satan comes and tempts you to do wrong? He makes you unhappy, and sometimes you get into trouble. I want to show you something that represents what Satan is like when he tries to get you in trouble. A pin! The point of a pin is very sharp—like Satan. His "pins" are very sharp, and he wants to destroy your happy life. So what happens when Satan comes into your life? Your balloon of happiness (pop the balloon). Did you know that Jesus has promised to be our Shield and will protect us from Satan? How many know what a shield is? I have one in my bag! What happens when Satan runs into the shield? (Hold the shield up to your chest for protection.) He can't break your happiness. He can't make you sin.

I hope each one of you will ask Jesus to be your Shield every day so that Satan can't take your happiness away. What you have to do is to pray and ask Jesus to protect you from Satan.

Diversity —Balloon 2

"But seek first his kingdom and his righteousness, and all these things will be given to you as well."
—Matthew 6:33, NIV

I have some things in my bag that are different sizes, shapes, and colors. Can you guess? *(Yes.)* OK, tell me. (Wait for the children's guesses.) Need more hints? Each one looks different, but they are all the same thing. Sometimes they are decorated with flowers. Sometimes you see them at parades or parties. Can you guess now? Balloons!

You boys and girls are a little like these balloons. Can you tell me why? (Let them respond.) You are all different in size, shape, and color, but you are all the same. How are you the same? All of you are God's children.

Do you like to play with balloons? Do you like to play with them when they look like this, when they are not yet blown up? No! What do they need? Air! How do we get air into the balloon? *(You just blow.)* (Hold the balloon down, and blow air from your mouth but not into the balloon. Respond to them when they say, "No" or "Not that way.") Something is wrong? OK, hold it against my mouth? (Blow again with the balloon on your lips but still not letting air into it.) It still doesn't work! What's wrong? OK, I see. I need to hold the balloon *in* my mouth and blow. (Now blow it up and hold it without letting the air out while you tell the rest of the story.)

How are these balloons like you in another way? How do you let God come into your life? You must study, pray, and ask Jesus to fill your life with His love! You can't love Jesus if you don't follow these steps. If you don't feel like praying to Jesus or reading your Bible, it is like letting the air out of the balloon. (Let the air out of the balloon.) You just shrivel up and lose your connection with Jesus.

I hope you boys and girls will remember to pray and to ask Jesus to fill you up.

Going Bananas!

"Do not be misled:
'Bad company corrupts good character.'"
—1 Corinthians 15:33, NIV

What You Need:
▶ two bananas—one with brown spots, one with a bruise on the inside

What I have in my bag today is sometimes long and sometimes short; sometimes it is green, and sometimes it is yellow. Can you guess what it is? *(Banana.)* Can you tell if a banana is good for eating by looking at the outside? Sometimes Yes, and sometimes No! Have you ever seen a banana that is yellow all over on the outside with *no* brown spots, but when you peeled it, it was bad on the inside? I did one time! I asked a man who worked with bananas why some bananas look great on the outside but are bruised on the inside. He said they were probably dropped when they were shipped—before they were ripe and yellow. Do you think a banana with brown spots is bad? Some people don't mind eating them even when they are bruised. Let's see what this banana is like on the inside.

Did you know that you boys and girls are a little like bananas? You can't always tell what they are like on the inside by the way they look on the outside. That is why you have to be careful when you pick your friends. Sometimes your parents may have to help you to know if someone will be a good friend for you.

Does God just look on our outside to see how good we look or how nice our clothes are? No! He looks on our inside, in our hearts and minds, to see if we really love Him. Just because we come to church doesn't mean that we really love Jesus.

I hope you will pray to Jesus every day to help you to be great on the inside and not to be so concerned about how pretty or how handsome you are on the outside. He loves you even if you have bruises, and He wants to take you to heaven to live with Him forever.

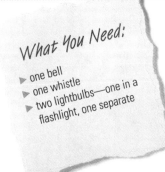

What You Need:

▶ one bell
▶ one whistle
▶ two lightbulbs—one in a flashlight, one separate

Listen Up!

"Peter said to him,
'We have left all we had to follow you!' "
—Luke 18:28, NIV

I have three things in my bag. Two of them make the same part of your body work, and the other one doesn't. Would you like to take a guess? *(It's too hard.)* Let me give you some clues. But first I want all of you to turn around. No looking! OK, wait until I have all three out before you guess.

Do you remember what I said about them? Two of them make the same part of your body work, but the third one doesn't need to use this part of your body.

(Bring out the lightbulb and the turned-on flashlight.) I am holding number one. *Do not look!* (Ring the bell.) OK, that is number two. Don't look yet. (Blow the whistle.) And that is number three. OK, you can turn around now to see what number one is.

Now you should know the answer to my question. What part of your body is used for two out of these three items? Your ears!

Did you know that some people can't hear a bell or a whistle? They can't hear when you talk to them. Your ears are a real blessing created by Jesus so that you can hear. Even though some people can't hear, they can learn to read lips or learn sign language so that they can talk to other people.

Can you always hear when someone talks to you? *(No, not always.)* (Talk without a sound.) Can you hear me now? *(No.)* Did I talk to you? *(Yes.)* Jesus talks to us the same way as I was just talking to you—so softly you couldn't hear me. We can't hear Him; but if we pray and listen, often we will know what He is telling us. He speaks to us through something very special that we are made with—*our consciences.* When you are tempted to do something you shouldn't do, is there some silent voice that tells you, "Don't do that"? That is called your conscience. Let me talk to you again. (Mouth the words *I love you.*) Did you hear me that time? No? Let me say it slowly in a different way. (Sign the words.)

Jesus will keep talking to you in *His* special way; and if you listen carefully, you will, through your conscience, know what He wants to tell you.

Big *G*, Little *g*

"You shall have no other gods before me."
—Exodus 20:3, NIV

Today I have several things in my bag to show you. Let's look at the first two. Can you read what the first one is? *(god.)* OK. What does the second one say? *(God.)* They both read the same thing, but can you tell me what the difference is between them? *(Big* G, *little* g!*)*

The big *G* in the word *God* is referring to our God in heaven, and the little *g* refers to all of the false gods people have made. When you read the Bible and you see the big *G* in the word *God*, you will always know it is talking about our God in heaven. Do you know what commandment tells us we only have *one* God? *(Yes, the second commandment.)*

Do you know what other gods are the little *g* gods? I have some in my bag. Would you like to see them? The first one is a statue of a Chinese god. Some people worship and pray to idols, also called statues. The second is an elephant. Some people worship live elephants, wooden elephants, stone elephants, or cloth pictures of elephants. Do you think these elephants can answer your prayers? *(No!)*

Can you tell me what this third idol is? *(Money.)* Some people spend all their time making or spending money and forget to spend time with *God.* There are lots of gods for each of us. Playing with your toys can be a god if you don't take the time to read your Bible and talk to God.

I hope each of you boys and girls will remember the second commandment and will remember we have only one *God.*

Let's say the commandment together. "You shall have no other gods before me" (Exodus, 20:3, NIV).

What You Need:

► four pieces of paper—a big *I* written on one, a little *i* on one, a big *U* on one, a little *u* on one

Big *I*, Little *i*; Big *U*, Little *u*

"So that from the rising of the sun to the place of its setting people may know there is none besides me. I am the LORD, and there is no other."

—Isaiah 45:6, NIV

oday I have some sheets of paper in my bag that I want to show you. They all have a letter from the alphabet on them. Can you tell me what letters are on these two pieces of paper? (Show the big *I* and little *i* sheets.) Can you tell me what the difference is between the two? *(Big I and little* i.*)*

Do you know of someone in the Bible who wanted to be the big *I*? *(Satan.)* Who did he want to be like? *(God.)* What do you see at the top of the little *i*? *(There is a dot on top.)* We need to be like the little *i*—always looking up to the top—as if the dot on the little *i* is like God. He is always on top and in the center.

I have two more sheets of paper. Can you tell me what letters these are, and what is different about the two letters? *(Big U and little* u.*)* Do both big and little letters look about the same? *(Yes.)* Both have two tall lines with a curved line that connects them together. They look like two *I*'s that are connected. One of the lines represents you, and the other represents God. If you let God come into your life every day, you will never want to be the big *I*. Even when you are a little *u*, you can be the same as a big *U*—just smaller. And you will be connected in the middle together with God.

God wants to be with you. Do you know how to ask Him to be in charge of your life? Pray and read your Bible. If you ask God to help you be a little *u* instead of a big *I*, then when He comes to take you to heaven, *u* (you and God) will go there together.

If that is what you would like, raise your hand. I want all of us to be there to listen to the stories that Jesus will tell us.

This Little Light of Mine!

▶ candles of different types—tea light, votive, birthday, dinner, etc.

"No one lights a lamp and then puts it under a basket. Instead, a lamp is placed on a stand, where it gives light to everyone in the house."
—Matthew 5:15, NLT

I have in my bag some things that have strings in the middle of them. They can be short, tall, skinny, or fat. The strings in them are called "wicks," and they are made from wax. Candles!

So there are lots of types of candles. Can you tell me what kind of candle this is? (Show a birthday candle.) *(Birthday.)* Yes. If we put this in the top of a birthday cake, will it be doing all that it can do? *(No.)* What do we do with it next? (Light it with a match.) Yes, someone needs to light it with a match! That is when a candle is most useful. Does a candle look good on a cake before it is lit? *(Yes.)* But does it look better after it is lit? *(Yes.)*

Did you know that you boys and girls are like birthday candles? Each one of you looks good. You are already very handsome or pretty; but when you let Jesus come into your life, you just light up. Jesus and His love will help you to shine brightly, and you will act and look better. With Jesus in your life, you will be happier; you will have a smile on your face; and you will not want to be disagreeable with your brothers and sisters, your friends, or your parents. Your time in Sabbath School and church will be happy.

A candle is *just* a little candle until someone lights it. A boy or girl is *just* a child until Jesus fills him or her with His love. That is the birth of Jesus in you. Jesus said, "You are the light of the world."

Are you ready for Jesus to make you like a bright-shining birthday candle?

Black Cover Bible

"All Scripture is inspired by God and is useful to teach us what is true and to make us realize what is wrong in our lives. It corrects us when we are wrong and teaches us to do what is right."
—2 Timothy 3:16, NLT

Before I show you what is in my bag today, I have some questions to ask you. OK, cover your eyes with your hands.

I have some pieces of paper in my hand. No peeking. Can you tell me what colors they are? *(No.)* (If they guess, say the following.) And were you peeking? Why can't you tell me the colors? *(Because our eyes are covered.)*

Let's try again. Uncover your eyes, and tell me what color you see now? (Show the black piece of paper.) *(Black.)* Yes!

Now keep your eyes open. Can you now tell me the colors of the pieces of paper in my hand? *(Yes.)*

OK. Do you want to see what is in my bag? It is a Bible with a black cover. Can you see what is inside the Bible? *(No.)* Why not? *(Because it is covered.)* You are so smart!

How can you see what is inside the Bible? (Open the cover.) Yes, just like when you uncovered your eyes and saw the colors of the papers.

Now if you open the Bible, can you read it or have your parents read it? *(Yes.)*

Some Bibles even have red print in them. Do you know what the red means? *(They are the words spoken by Jesus.)* You are right!

I hope each of you will remember that when you see a Bible, in order to know what is inside, you have to *open* the cover and read it. Once you read the words in it, you will know all the wonderful things Jesus wants us to know about Him and His Father, God. Read some every day!

Powered Up by Jesus

What You Need:
➤ the cover of a good book or magazine
➤ one smaller book or magazine that fits inside of the cover of the first book
➤ three flashlights—one with batteries, two without batteries

"If any of you lacks wisdom, you should ask God, who gives generously to all without finding fault, and it will be given to you."
—James 1:5, NIV

In my bag today is something most boys and girls use often—especially if they are in school. Some are big, and some are small; some are thick, and some are thin. What do you think I have? *(Book or magazine.)* Raise your hand if you like to read or to have your parents read to you. Good!

Have you ever heard someone say, "You can't judge a book by its cover"? Do you know what that means? (Let the children respond.) It means you can't always tell what is on the inside by looking at the cover. Let me show you this book (magazine). It looks good and interesting on the outside, but it doesn't look as good on the inside.

Would you like to see what else is in my bag that will help you to understand what that phrase means? *(Flashlights.)* I need helpers to hold these, but do not turn them on yet. (Choose one child for each flashlight you have.) Which one do you think will shine the brightest? Can you tell by the size or color of the flashlight? At the count of three, turn them on and let's see! (Count out loud, then turn them on.) Why is the smallest one the brightest? (Let the children respond.) It is the only one that works! Why don't you think the others work? Let's see why. *(The smallest one is the only one that has batteries.)* Right! It is the *power* inside that makes the light shine.

When you are choosing a friend, do you check out how they are "powered" first? We have to choose our friends carefully. They may dress nicely or have expensive toys. But are they powered with Jesus on the inside? We can't judge other boys and girls, but we can ask Jesus to help us pick good friends. We also need to ask Jesus to put His power inside us so that others can see we are Christians who love Him—just like the flashlight has power inside it from the batteries.

How many of you boys and girls want to have Jesus' *power* inside of you? (Read 1 Samuel 16:7.)

What You Need:

▸ one bucket
▸ seven pieces of paper
  with one word on each—
  Love, Joy, Peace, Faith,
  Meekness, Temperance,
  Goodness—folded and
  placed in the bucket

Bucket List

"I pray that God, the source of hope, will fill you completely with joy and peace because you trust in him. Then you will overflow with confident hope through the power of the Holy Spirit."
—Romans 15:13, NLT

There is something in my bag that has something else on the inside of it. What I have can be either big or small, can be different colors, and usually has a handle on it. Want to take a guess? *(A bucket.)* How can a bucket be used? (Let the children guess.) *(To fill with sand at the beach, to fill with water, to fill with fruit from a tree, etc.)*

This bucket has something else in it. Let's take a look. There are pieces of paper. The papers have words written on them. Let's read them. (Remove them one at a time and have a different child read each word: *love, joy, peace, faith, meekness, temperance, goodness.*) Do these words describe what you are like on the inside?

What happens when someone you are playing with is unkind to you or takes something that belongs to you? Does that take the *love* and *joy* from your heart? There are boys and girls who like to do unkind things, which will remove the *love* and *joy* from your bucket.

Jesus has promised to fill our buckets every day with these good things *if* we love Him and ask Him to fill our "buckets"—our hearts and minds—with them.

It makes us happier when kids are nice to us. They are the ones who fill up your buckets. If you ask Jesus, He will help you fill other boys' and girls' buckets with love and joy and all the other words we found in the bucket today.

Begin every day by asking Jesus to help you fill your bucket with good things and to help you fill someone else's bucket as well. He wants to bless you with all of these good things.

Building Blocks

"Look! I stand at the door and knock.
If you hear my voice and open the door, I will come in,
and we will share a meal together as friends."
—Revelation 3:20, NLT

What You Need:
- colored building blocks of different shapes
- one Bible
- children's devotional books

I have several things in my bag to show you today. Would you like to see them? (Take one building block from the bag.) Do you know what this is? *(Building block.)* What can you do with it? You can't do much because there is only one. (Bring out several more, and put them on top of the first one.) Is this better? *(A little.)* Can we do anything with the different colors and shapes? (Start to build something.) We still need more, don't we? (Bring out the remaining blocks.) This is a lot better, right? Can we build something with all of these? Yes, we can build a lot of different things.

Can anyone tell me what day New Year's falls on? (If close to New Year's Day, ask how many days ago it was.) That's right, January 1. That is a special day because we can build (start) a new year just like we can build something new and different with these blocks.

I want to show you some other building blocks that you should use every day. What is this one? *(The Bible.)* This book contains God's words that help us learn how He wants us to live. What are these? *(Daily devotional books?)* There are interesting stories about other people in them, which help us learn to stay close to Jesus. There is one more building block that I can't show you, but you know how to do it. Can you guess what is? *(Prayer!)* Prayer is the time we can talk to Jesus and thank Him for all He does for us. I hope each of you will use your building blocks every day.

(This story fits New Year's Day or any other time because tomorrow is another day, and with God you can begin over again at any time.)

What You Need:
- one sheet of paper
- cardboard to back the paper
- one dart or arrow
- one compass that shows direction
- one compass for drawing circles

Bull's-Eye

"But the gateway to life is very narrow and the road is difficult, and only a few ever find it."
—Matthew 7:14, NLT

What do you suppose I have in my bag today? I have a piece of paper, and I have something that is metal with a pencil attached. Would you like to see them? Here is the piece of paper, and here is a compass. Oh, and here is another compass!

Let me tell you about the difference between this compass (Show one compass.) and this compass. (Show the other.) This compass helps you to find the direction you are going when you get lost. So what do you think this compass is used for? *(Making circles.)* Yes! You can move the pencil closer or farther from the center, which will make circles of a different size, like this.

Have any of you ever used this kind of compass? Let me show you how to use it. (Draw a large circle on the paper.) What is this? *(A circle.)* How would you describe the shape of this circle? *(It is round.)* Now I am going to draw a smaller circle that starts in the center of the bigger circle. (Place your compass tip in the middle, and draw a series of smaller circles to make a bull's-eye.)

Do you know what this is? (Let the children respond.) This is called a "bull's-eye!" Do you know how to use a bull's-eye? *(It's a target for darts, a bow and arrow, or a gun.)* When you use a bull's-eye, what do you aim for? *(The middle of the smallest circle.)* When you hit that area, it means you are a good shot. If you miss and hit the larger circles, it means you need more practice.

Now, what does this compass and bull's-eye have to do with your life? Matthew 7:14 states that the path to heaven is straight and narrow. That is like hitting the small circle in the bull's-eye. If I want to hit the center of the bull's-eye, can I throw the dart in the wrong direction? (Act like you're going to throw it away from the bull's-eye.) *(No!)* In what direction do I have to throw it? *(Straight toward the bull's-eye!)*

That is how Jesus wants us to live our lives—to keep our eyes focused on Him. How do we do that? We pray; we read our Bibles, where we learn that Jesus promises to forgive us when we do wrong. If we hit the center of the bull's-eye one time, should we stop practicing? *(No!)* We will lose the skill of our aim if we do not practice. If we only pray to Jesus once, does that mean we can stop praying? *(No!)* We need to continue praying to Jesus every day so that Satan cannot tempt us to forget about Jesus. He is your Helper.

Candles of Three Generations

What You Need:
➤ three candles (burned a little)—one tall, one shorter, one very short

"In the same way, let your good deeds shine out for all to see, so that everyone will praise your heavenly Father."
—Matthew 5:16, NLT

have three things in my bag that I want to show you, but first I want to tell you something. And then I have a question for you.

Raise your hand if you have grandparents. Is it fun to spend time with them? Do they do nice things for you? Sometimes your parents think your grandparents spoil you. That just means they think your grandma and grandpa give you more than you need at times.

We are going to talk about a big word. The word is *generation*! Does anyone know what that word means? A *generation* is a layer of family. OK, that is still hard to understand, so let me explain by asking you a question. How many generations are there when you count your grandparents, your parents, and yourself? (Show a finger for each generation.) *(Three.)* That's right!

I have something in my bag that represents three generations. (Remove the three candles.) Are they all the same? Look at them closely. All three are different sizes. If these represent three generations, from the oldest to the youngest, which one represents you? The tallest one, the smaller one, or the shortest one? (Wait for their response.) You are the tallest one. Surprised? Let me explain.

What do we use candles for? *(To see light! Not birthday candles.)* If I was to light all three of these candles right now, which one will take the longest time to burn out? *(The tallest one!)* That is why it represents you. Your grandparents have lived a lot longer than you and have let their light shine for many years. They don't have as many years left to let their light shine as you have. Because they have let their light shine for many years, they are looking forward to living in heaven forever when Jesus comes.

Who wants to live in heaven with Jesus? You can be ready by letting your "light" shine every day. Begin by telling your friends and family how much Jesus loves them.

What You Need:
▶ one red-and-white-striped candy cane

Christmas Candy Cane 1

"But he was pierced for our transgressions, he was crushed for our iniquities; the punishment that brought us peace was on him, and by his wounds we are healed."

—Isaiah 53:5, NIV

I have something in my bag that is red and white. It has stripes. Want to guess? Do you need another clue? If you turn it upside down, it makes the shape of the letter *J. (Candy cane.)*

Did you know a candy cane is more than just a sweet treat at Christmas? There is a story that I found several years ago about the candy cane and what each part means. I would like to tell the story to you.

Its shape is like a shepherd's staff. Its red stripes remind us that Jesus shed His blood for us, and "by his wounds we are healed" (Isaiah 53:5, NIV). Its white stripes stand for purity, and by His death we are made pure. This means that because He died for our sins, He took them and left us clean of our sins (white as snow). The peppermint flavor is very much like hyssop, a plant that tastes like mint and that was used in Bible times for making things clean or pure. It's called "purification." (Read Psalm 51:7, NIV.) The candy cane's taste is sweet, as it is sweet to walk with Jesus. Turn the candy cane upside down, and it becomes a *J* for Jesus!

Carbon Paper

"Those who say they live in God
should live their lives as Jesus did."
—1 John 2:6, NLT

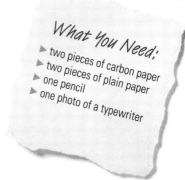

What You Need:
- two pieces of carbon paper
- two pieces of plain paper
- one pencil
- one photo of a typewriter

I have something in my bag that by itself isn't very pretty. By itself, it is of no use. However you mark it, it shows the same mark on whatever it touches. Have I confused you? You probably won't know what it is because you may have never seen something like this. Just in case you may have, I will give you a few more clues. Sometimes it is black, and sometimes it is blue or sometimes other colors. Give up? It is carbon paper! The piece I have is black; and as you can see, it doesn't look very pretty. Do you know what it is used for? To copy what you write, draw, or type on it; it copies that same thing to the piece of paper behind it or to whatever you want to transfer it to.

A long time ago, before we had computers and copy machines, there were typewriters. (Show photo.) When you typed a letter and wanted a copy of the letter, you had to put a piece of carbon paper between the two pieces of paper. Now you just type on the computer, click Print, and get as many copies as you want.

Did you know that you boys and girls are sometimes like carbon paper? If you say bad words to other kids, they may copy what you have said. If you say good things, they may copy those good things as well.

Let's see how the carbon paper works! (Write *bad* in big letters on the top of the paper.) What do you see on the original piece of paper and on the copy? (Show them both.) You see the exact same word. (Now write *good*.) What do you see this time? Again, the same word! Do you see how you can be like carbon paper? You need to be careful how you talk and act because others may follow your actions or words. Do you want to talk and act like Satan or like Jesus? I believe all of you would rather be like Jesus!

If we say something that isn't nice and then are sorry for what we said and ask forgiveness, Jesus has promised to take that sin away (1 John 1:9). What that means is He will tear up the *carbon paper* of your life, and your sin will be gone. (Tear up the carbon paper, and throw it away.) Every day after you have asked Jesus to forgive your sins, you will start the day with a clean piece of carbon paper—like this one. Start each day this way, and you will be acting like Jesus.

Christmas Candy Cane 2

"For to us a child is born, to us a son is given, and the government will be on his shoulders. And he will be called Wonderful Counselor, Mighty God, Everlasting Father, Prince of Peace."
—Isaiah 9:6, NIV

What special day is coming soon? *(Christmas.)* What makes Christmas so special? (Let children respond.) *(Family, presents, Jesus' birth.)* What is the most important? *(Jesus' birth.)*

I wonder if you think I forgot to talk about what is in my bag today. I haven't! Would you like a clue? What is in my bag is sometimes long and sometimes short, but it always has a bend at the top. Can you guess? It's a candy cane. Who likes candy canes? There are lots of stories about candy canes, but I want to tell you what I think of when I see one. I hope you will remember this.

Who can tell me what the red stripe reminds them of? There are two things. The first is *sin*. The Bible says your sins are like scarlet—or bright red. The second is Jesus' blood. Because Jesus gave His life for our sins, the red represents His blood that takes our sins away. The white stripe reminds us of the way we look after Jesus has forgiven our sins. We are white like snow. The bend at the top of a real cane is used by a shepherd when he guides a lamb back to the flock with the crook in the cane. That also reminds me that Jesus is always trying to pull us closer to Him. All we have to do is follow.

If Jesus had not been born, we would not have Christmas. Jesus is God's Gift to us. The candy cane reminds us of Jesus' love for each one of you boys and girls. He wants you to ask Him to make you "white as snow" by forgiving your sins so that He can welcome you to heaven when He comes to take us there.

I want to give each one of you a Christmas present that I hope will remind you every time you see a candy cane that Jesus wants to make you pure, like the white stripe in the candy.

Christmas Presents and Measuring Cups

What You Need:
➤ four measuring cups
➤ one Bible

"Give, and you will receive. Your gift will return to you in full—pressed down, shaken together to make room for more, running over, and poured into your lap. The amount you give will determine the amount you get back."
—Luke 6:38, NLT

What special holiday is coming soon? Have you decided what you are giving to Jesus? Have you decided on the presents you will give to your parents? Have you written down what presents you want to receive? Christmas is a special day when we celebrate the best Gift we have ever received—the gift of Jesus. He is the reason for celebrating Christmas. Never forget that!

I haven't forgotten to tell you what is in my bag today. I need helpers. There are four things in my bag. (Remove one.) What is this? *(A measuring cup.)* Right. Let's get the other three out of the bag. Who can tell me what these four things have in common? How are they alike? *(They all measure amounts.)* Is measuring important? How do you think the cookies that your parents make would taste if they didn't measure the sugar, didn't count how many eggs they added, and didn't measure the water they added to the bowl? Do you think the cookies would taste good?

What if someone told you to get as much candy as you could hold in one hand? Would you try to pack your hand full? Did you know there is a verse in the Bible where Jesus talks about measuring something? Listen as I read Luke 6:38. "Give, and you will receive. Your gift will return to you in full—pressed down, shaken together to make room for more, running over, and poured into your lap. The amount you give will determine the amount you get back" (NLT). Jesus is talking about what happens when you have a giving heart. He says that if you give, you will receive many gifts in return. Not necessarily things, but giving to others makes your heart happy.

The best gift you could give to Jesus is yourself. Don't forget that *you* are what He would like most from you. Remember your mom and dad. They like gifts that you make—maybe a pretty picture, a promise to clean your room every day. Parents like those gifts. What if you ask your parents if you can do some jobs to earn money to buy a present for someone who may not otherwise get one? Giving is fun!

What You Need:
▶ one pair of men's pants
▶ one ladies' dress

Clothes Don't Fit

"And the boy Samuel continued to grow in stature
and in favor with the LORD and with people."
—1 Samuel 2:26, NIV

I have two items in my bag today. One is for a male and one for a female. Do you have any ideas? (Let the children respond.) I think you need some clues. I will tell you that all boys have the items meant for males, and all girls have the items meant for females. Need another clue? They are items to be worn. *(Clothes.)* I need a volunteer boy and a volunteer girl. Young man, I would like you to put on this pair of pants. And young lady, I would like you to put on this dress. Let's see how you look. What's the problem? *(They don't fit.)* How come? *(They are too big.)* Oh, it looks like you will have to grow into them; the pants are a man's size, and the dress is a woman's size. You'll have to grow up before you can wear them, right?

Do you think you are a grown-up Christian? (Let them respond.) That means you would know everything about Jesus. I don't think so! Do you think all of the grown-ups in here know everything there is to know about being a Christian? I don't think so!

In order for you boys and girls to grow, what are some of the things you have to do? (Let them respond.) You have to eat, sleep, exercise, drink water, and get fresh air and sunshine. How do we grow up knowing Jesus better? (Let them respond.) You need to read your Bibles, study your Sabbath School lessons, learn your memory verses, and pray every day.

Many people say Jesus is coming soon, and I believe that. I know each one of you wants to see Jesus. I pray you will remember to grow up with Jesus daily, just like you are growing up to fit into larger clothes.

"Son" Shine

What You Need:
➤ two containers of water
➤ blue and yellow food coloring

"Yet to all who did receive him, to those who believed in his name, he gave the right to become children of God."
—John 1:12, NIV

I have two containers in my bag. They both contain the same ingredients, but they don't look the same. (Show the blue water container.) So what is in this glass? *(Colored water.)* Have you ever heard people say they are feeling blue? Do you know what that means? When people say they are "blue," it means they are sad or unhappy. When you have done something wrong and you feel sorry for what you have done, you can say, "I am blue."

What color is this one? *(Yellow.)* Can you tell me something that is yellow? *(Someone might say the sun.)* How do you spell *sun?* Do you know another word that sounds the same but is spelled differently and means something different? *(Son.)* Jesus is the *Son* of God! His love is warm just like the sun is warm.

Let's pretend this jar represents the *Son,* Jesus. Do you know what happens to us when we let the Son into our blue lives? Let's see. (Pour the liquid from one container into the other.) Look. The blue is gone! We can be happy! What color is the water now? Green! What do you think of when you see the color green? *(Grass, leaves, trees.)* What is something else that we see on the road that is green? A green light, which means "go!"

When we let Jesus come into our lives, He will let us go to heaven. Raise your hand if you want to go to heaven. Jesus removes the "blue" when we ask Him to forgive our sins.

What You Need:

▸ one combination lock with instructions
▸ a small item that can be locked, with the word Sin written on it
▸ one Bible

Combination Lock

"Listen to my instruction and be wise;
do not disregard it."
—Proverbs 8:33, NIV

H ow many of you boys and girls have ever been locked in or out of somewhere? (Let the children respond.) How did you get in or out? *(Unlocked the door.)* Today I have a lock in my bag. A lock has a very important lesson for you.

Raise your hand if you are a Christian. Good; all of you are! Do you want to see my lock? Do you know what kind of lock this is? It's called a "combination lock." It seems to be locked on to this piece of (wood, metal, or plastic). Who can read the word on it? *(Sin!)*

How can we unlock this *sin* from the lock? What can we use? *(Key, saw, bolt cutters, numbers.)* Numbers! Does it matter what numbers we should use? *(Yes.)* Where can we learn what the correct numbers are? *(From the instructions.)* I have the instructions, and I see the three numbers: ## - ## - ##. Good. We should be able to open the lock now. *Hmm.* This dial turns both right and left. Do you think it matters which way we turn it first? *(Yes. No.)* (Try turning it as the children suggest. Stop on the first number, and then ask which way should be next.) *Hmm!* Does it matter how many times I turn the dial each way? *(Yes. No.)* I guess I better read *all* of the instructions. OK, it says, (read the directions aloud). It opened! So if we have the directions and follow them, we can unlock the lock and remove the *sin.*

Jesus has given us an instruction Book to help us grow up to be happy Christians. Do you know what that instruction Book is called? *(Bible.)* (Show the children the Bible.) The Bible will show us how to unlock sin from our lives!

Do you remember which direction the instructions said to turn the dial first? *(Right.)* That is the same direction we have to turn. Right, not wrong. If we make *wrong* choices, Jesus can't live in our hearts. But if we make the *right* choices and ask Jesus to forgive our sins, He will gladly live in our hearts. Just like we followed the instructions for the lock, we should follow the instructions in the Bible for a happy life with Jesus. Jesus is waiting to enter our hearts. All we have to do is ask Him in prayer. I hope every time you see a combination lock, you will remember you must turn *right* to get away from sin. The *right* turn will lead to heaven.

Big Word—Conscience

"The goal of this command is love, which comes from a pure heart and a good conscience and a sincere faith."

—1 Timothy 1:5, NIV

You boys and girls often know the answers to my questions. I am very proud of you for being so smart. Today I want to talk about a *big* word! I want to be sure you know what it means. The word is *conscience.* Can anyone tell me what that word means? *(A feeling or knowledge of right and wrong.)* Where does that feeling come from? *(God.)*

An Indian boy was asked that question a long time ago. He replied, "A little three-cornered thing is my conscience. It stands still when I am good; but when I am bad it turns and squirms, and the corners hurt very much. If I keep on doing wrong, however, by and by the corners wear away, and then it hurts no more."

Do you think that is a good explanation of *conscience?* In my bag, I have something that is a good example of how this boy answered the question. Would you like to see it? It's a stone with sharp points. If you put it in your pocket, it will keep sticking into your leg when you walk. It may even wear a hole in your pocket. Have you ever gotten a small rock in your shoe? Did it hurt when you would walk? How about a little bit of sand?

What about this rock? Where do you think it came from? It is called a river rock. It is smooth because as the water runs over and over it, it rubs against other rocks until all the sharp points are smooth. This is like the Indian boy's story. If you continue to do wrong, the sharp points will wear off and won't hurt anymore. Then it will be easier to keep doing wrong things.

God has given us many helpers who teach us how to make good choices. Can you name some? *(Parents, teachers, pastors, police officers.)* The most important helper that God has given us is the Bible. It teaches us about our conscience by guiding us to make good decisions.

Cooking Oil and Water

"If we confess our sins to him, he is faithful and just
to forgive us our sins and to cleanse us from all wickedness."
—1 John 1:9, NLT

There are two items in my bag that are somewhat the same but are different. Let me give you some clues. One is yellow, and the other is clear. One you can drink, and the other you wouldn't want to drink. *(Oil and water.)* How are they the same? *(Both are liquids.)* How are they different? (Let the children respond.)

I want to show you something interesting about them. Have any of you ever sinned? *(Yes.)* Let's pretend this oil is sin and represents you and me. Because the oil is light colored, we will consider it little sins. Some people think sins such as lying or cheating are just little sins. But sin is sin!

(Show the water jar.) Let's pretend this jar of water is Jesus—crystal-clear, with no sins! Let's see what happens when we put a little "Jesus" (water jar) into us (oil jar). (Pour the water into the oil.) *Hmm.* The oil and water don't mix together. They stay separated. Does Jesus mix with the sin we have? *(No.)* That means we need to be sure we have no sins that haven't been forgiven. Right? So how do we get rid of the sin? First John 1:9 states, "If we confess our sins to him, he is faithful and just to forgive us our sins and to cleanse us from all wickedness" (NLT).

How can each of you boys and girls keep Jesus in your life? *(Prayer, Bible study, Sabbath School lesson study, going to church and Sabbath School.)* Yes, there are lots of things you can do to keep Jesus in your life.

Let's see what happens when we put more of Jesus into us! (Pour more water into the oil.) What comes out first? Sin! When we ask Jesus to forgive us and fill us up with Him, He removes the sin from us.

How many of you boys and girls want Jesus to fill you to the top and make you clean from sin?

Coupons

What You Need:
► shopping coupons

"Submit yourselves, then, to God.
Resist the devil, and he will flee from you."
—James 4:7, NIV

What I have in my bag today is something you can get for free! Wow. There isn't much you can get for free these days, is there? Need a clue? (Show the children the coupons.) They are just little pieces of paper with items printed on them. If you use one, you can save some money on a product when you buy it. They are called "coupons." Have you ever seen your mother or father use coupons at the store? The companies that give them to you have learned that if they give you free coupons that will save you money, you might buy their products instead of someone else's products. Some coupons are good, but some are for things that you can get cheaper from another brand.

Did you know that Satan wants to tempt us to eat or do things that he thinks we would probably like after trying them? The Bible tells us there are some things we should not eat because they are not good for us, but Satan tempts us with those things. Remember when Satan told Eve it was OK to eat the fruit that God said not to eat?

Satan does the same thing with you and me. He tempts people to smoke cigarettes, drink alcohol, and use drugs. He does the same thing with bad movies, bad games, and bad words. Who should we believe—Satan or Jesus? Satan tries to make bad things look good. He wants you to think it doesn't matter what you do, that it's OK, and that you still can go to heaven.

The only way we can know if something is good or bad is to pray and ask Jesus to show us the difference. Remember that Satan is always trying to influence you to think it is OK to do things that Jesus doesn't want you to do. Don't listen to Satan!

What You Need:

▶ one cucumber grown inside a bottle

Cucumber in a Bottle

"There is a way that appears to be right, but in the end it leads to death."
—Proverbs 16:25, NIV

Have any of you ever been locked in a room or a car? Was it easy to get out? Let me ask you another question. Have any of you ever done something you shouldn't have done and been caught? Did you get into trouble? Was it fun to be in trouble?

Who can tell me what the word *habit* means? Are there good and bad habits? Can you tell me some good habits? (Let the children respond.) What about bad habits? (Let them respond.) Is it easy to start a habit? Is it easy to break (stop) a habit? Sometimes it is easy to break a good habit, such as remembering to brush your teeth, after you eat, to keep you from getting cavities. Sometimes you don't want to do it, even though you know it is important, so you stop doing it. But we should keep our good habits. What about the bad habits, such as playing video games that are not good to play? Because you like to play those games, you develop a bad habit. That is a habit you should break (stop).

I have something in my bag that is like a habit. Would you like to see it? Do you know what it is? (*A cucumber in a bottle.*) How could a cucumber in a bottle be compared to a bad habit? (*It was easy for the cucumber to start growing in the bottle, but now you can't get it out!*) Do you think it was a good idea for the farmer to plant a cucumber in a bottle? (*No!*) Was there a way to keep it from growing after it was put in the bottle? (*No!*) It just kept growing and growing.

That is how it is like a *bad* habit. It is easy to begin a bad habit; but once it starts it is hard to stop it! So when you are tempted to start a bad habit, I hope you will remember this cucumber in the bottle. How can you avoid starting a bad habit? Pray to Jesus for help! He can help you and is anxious to have you in heaven with Him. How many of you boys and girls want to go to heaven?

Cup—Full to the Brim

What You Need:
- one bottle of water to fill empty cup
- one large coffee mug or teacup

"So do not fear, for I am with you; do not be dismayed,
for I am your God. I will strengthen you and help you;
I will uphold you with my righteous right hand."
—Isaiah 41:10, NIV

have something in my bag that is sometimes easy to carry and sometimes not so easy. It is something that you would use for a hot drink. Can you guess what it might be? *(A teacup.)* Can you drink anything else from a teacup besides tea? *(Yes!)* What is your favorite thing to drink from a teacup?

Did you know in England a teacup is something special? Do you know why? In England, there is an activity simply known as "tea." It works like this. You might get a call from a friend who would ask, "Can you come for tea this afternoon?" That means a little more than just a cup of tea. People get together for tea and crumpets (a special pastry). The teacups are very fancy, and the ladies hold their teacups daintily, like this. (Show the children how.) I need a helper. OK, you are big enough to hold this teacup. Let's pretend I am pouring you a cup of tea. We will fill it about half full. Can you still hold it? No problem? Good! Let's see if you can get up and walk with it without spilling it. Very good! Now let's try something different. Let's fill it all the way up to the brim (the top). Now can you walk without spilling it? (Let the child try.) That is harder. What if I had helped you? Would it have been easier if I poured the tea into a larger cup? *(Yes.)* Sometimes we need help to do certain things!

Do you boys and girls ever need help? Tell me some of the things you need help with. (Let the children respond.) Who helps you with these things? Let's pretend that you are trying to carry a large, heavy cup, and it is full to the top, just like we did today. Maybe you said, "I can do it by myself." As you get bigger and stronger, you will be able to do more things by yourself. Right now though, when you try to do something by yourself that is too difficult, you will probably make a mess and then have to clean it up. You should have asked for help!

Did you know that Jesus is always waiting at your side to help you when you get into a mess? When you sin, tell Jesus you are sorry and ask Him to forgive you. As you grow up, I hope you will remember how Jesus has always forgiven you whenever you asked for His help. Remember the teacup filled to the brim when you need help. Jesus is always there for you.

What You Need:
▸ a large supply of dimes

Dimes

"For it is by grace you have been saved, through faith—and this is not from yourselves, it is the gift of God—not by works, so that no one can boast."
—Ephesians 2:8, 9, NIV

What I have in my bag today is something that can be used to buy something—but not very much. Can you guess what it is? *(Dimes.)* Can you buy much with just a dime (ten cents)? Let me ask you some questions.

How many of you boys and girls try to do what is right? I am glad to see all of your hands! How many of you *always* do what is right? If we always did what was right, we would be perfect, and Jesus is the only One who lived a perfect life. So if we aren't perfect, does that mean we must have made mistakes? The Bible says all have sinned—everyone but Jesus.

By the way, what is *sin*? Can you think of some things that are sins? (Let the children respond.) If you tell a lie, is that a sin? What if you take something that doesn't belong to you—is that a sin? Have you heard of the Ten Commandments? One of those commandments says, "Thou shalt not steal." It sounds like stealing is a sin, right? Jesus gave us guidelines in the Ten Commandments to help us know what is right and what is wrong.

What if your parents gave you a dime (ten cents) every time you sinned? Do you think you could get quite a lot of money? What would you do with all the money you earned from sinning? You could buy a lot of toys and things that would be fun to play with. But getting money for a sin would not make you happy.

How many dimes would you have to give Jesus to take you to heaven if you saved a lot of dimes? *(All of them?)* Well, I have good news. Jesus doesn't want your dimes. You cannot pay Him to take you to heaven. Heaven is a free gift, just like our Bible verse states. All He wants is for you to be truly sorry for what you did wrong and to ask Him to forgive you. Jesus wants to take you to heaven when He comes. What you have to do is ask Him to help you to not sin.

Dirty Water and Clean Water

What You Need:
- one pan
- one jar of dirty water
- one jar of clean water
- dirty hands
- one towel

"Finally, brothers and sisters, whatever is true, whatever is noble, whatever is right, whatever is pure, whatever is lovely, whatever is admirable—if anything is excellent or praiseworthy—think about such things."
—Philippians 4:8, NIV

If you have dirty hands, do you need something to help get them clean? Are my hands dirty? Do I have something in my bag that will help? Actually, I have three things that will help. You will probably use at least two of them, but only one is necessary. Can you guess what it is? *(Water.)*

Let's see what I have in my bag. A pan to wash in! A good thing to have, but can you wash your hands with a pan? *(No.)* What do you need in the pan? *(Water.)* Right. Let's see what else I have. A jar of really dirty water! Would you want to wash your hands in this water? I thought you said I need water. Well, this is water! Won't this make my hands clean? *(No!)*

Remember I said I have three things in my bag? What do you think the third thing is? *(Clear water.)* Will this get my hands clean? Can I wash with this water? *(Yes!)*

Do you take a bath just once a month? *(No!)* How about once a week? *(No!)* It's nice to be able to take a bath every day because it feels good to be clean. Isn't it nice to be clean?

Let me ask another question. Raise your hand if you like to watch TV or movies or to play games. That many of you? There are some good things to see. There are also many bad things on TV, in movies, and in games. Things you shouldn't watch or play. It is like these two jars of water. Some are like the dirty water, and some are like the clean. I hope you will remember these two jars of water, which represent the good and bad choices you can make. Remember to choose the clean-water choices. If we ask Him, Jesus will help you choose the good TV programs, the good movies, and the good games.

What You Need:

▶ one dishonest-fisherman's ruler (one side is ten inches long, the other side is twenty inches long)

Dishonest Ruler

"Truthful lips endure forever,
but a lying tongue lasts only a moment."
—Proverbs 12:19, NIV

Have any of you boys and girls ever been fishing? Did you catch anything? How long was it? Have you ever heard someone tell about a *big* fish that got away? Sometimes people say the fish they caught was bigger than it actually was. Is that telling the truth? *(No.)*

Would you like to see what I have in my bag that some people might try to use when telling their fish stories? This is my dishonest-fisherman's ruler. Can you see how many inches long it is? *(Twenty inches.)* Does this look twenty inches long?

Let's look at the other side. Right here it states, "For the honest fisherman!" What does *honest* mean? *(Telling the truth.)* It is ten inches long. If I caught a fish that measured as ten inches long but I used the dishonest ruler, would you believe me if I said it were twenty inches? *(No!)* Is it OK to lie? *(No!)* Would it be OK for you to tell all your friends that I told a lie—even if I were joking with you? *(No.)*

Jesus told us in the ninth commandment not to lie or say bad things about other boys or girls to your friends. Jesus only wants us to say good things and to tell the truth. I hope each one of you will remember the dishonest ruler the next time you start to say something that is not true.

Dog Leash

What You Need:
▸ one dog leash

"When Jesus spoke again to the people, he said,
'I am the light of the world. Whoever follows me will never
walk in darkness, but will have the light of life.' "
—John 8:12, NIV

I have something in my bag that you can use if you are following or if you are leading something or someone. It can be short or long and sometimes comes in different colors. Can you guess? Have any of you ever taken a dog for a walk? Now can you guess? *(A leash.)* Does the dog always walk beside you and go in the direction you want it to go? *(No.)* If the dog decides it wants to go in a different direction and doesn't go where it is supposed to go, what do you do? *(Tug on its leash.)* Dogs sometimes decide to go their own way even though you are leading them a different way. Dogs are smart, and I wonder if they know they are disobeying your instructions. I think so!

How would you feel if your parents were to put a leash around you to pull you where they want you to go—especially if you didn't want to go that way? You wouldn't like that, would you? No, that wouldn't be fun at all. Aren't you glad they don't do that? If they were to do that, would you be able to choose what you wanted to do or where you wanted to go? No, of course not! Do you think your parents are trying to control you when they tell you what you should or should not do? Do you think they do it to be mean, or do you think they do it because they love you so much that they want you to grow up to be kind, responsible, and loving men and women who will make good choices?

Who can tell me what a shepherd does? A shepherd watches his or her flock of sheep all day and night. The sheep follow the shepherd. If one sheep goes in a different direction, the shepherd goes after it and brings it back. Do you think the shepherd has to put a leash on each sheep? No, the sheep know their shepherd loves them, and they will follow the shepherd wherever he or she leads them. If they are lost, the shepherd has a long staff with a bend at the end (the same shape as a candy cane) to reach them and bring them back into the fold.

The people who take care of you are like shepherds. They love you and want you to go in the direction that will make you happiest, and that is to follow Jesus.

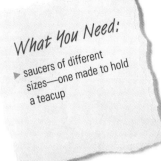

Drinking From a Saucer

"Give, and it will be given to you. A good measure, pressed down, shaken together and running over, will be poured into your lap. For with the measure you use, it will be measured to you."
—Luke 6:38, NIV

I have several things in my bag that are all called by the same name but that all look a little different. Do you need some clues? All of them are round; some are different colors, some are glass, and some are plastic. Do you have any ideas? *Hmm.* This is a hard one to guess. They are saucers!

One of these saucers is special because it holds a teacup. (Show the children.) How can you tell it is for a teacup? It has a little indented space in the center to hold the cup. Why is the indent so special? Without it, the teacup can slide around. Have you ever seen someone drink from a teacup? Some people just pick up the cup and drink from it. Others hold the saucer under the cup while they lift it, so if they spill any tea, it will be caught in the saucer. Have you ever seen someone drink from the saucer? Sometimes people will pour a little tea into the saucer and drink from it. Why do you think they do that? Some say it tastes better that way; some say it helps to cool the tea so that they don't burn their tongues; and some say they do it just for fun.

There is a song titled "Fill My Cup, Lord." What do you think that means? It is like you asking Jesus to fill your life full of blessings. What are some of the blessings that Jesus has given you or someone you love? (Let the children respond.) Do you ever ask Jesus to bless your parents? What about your friends?

I hope you will pray that Jesus will fill your cup—your life—full of blessings. If your cup gets too full, I hope that you will share what spills over with your friends and family.

Empty Gift Box

What You Need:
▶ one empty Christmas-
wrapped box

"Trust in the LORD with all your heart and lean not on
your own understanding; in all your ways submit to him,
and he will make your paths straight."
—Proverbs 3:5, 6, NIV

Who can tell me what special holiday is coming up soon? *(Christmas.)* Why is Christmas special? *(Presents received and given, family gatherings, the birth of Jesus.)* Yes, Jesus makes Christmas very special. And yes, you will have nice gifts that also make it special. Do you ever ask your parents or family for a specific gift? For something you really want? Do you pray for that gift also?

I want to show you something that is in my bag. Would you like to see what it is? A present all wrapped up for Christmas! Shall we look inside the present? Let's open it! Wow! What a disappointment! There is nothing inside the box. Should we be sad when we don't get what we asked and prayed for?

Do you know that some of God's *best gifts* are prayers not answered the way we want them answered? Jesus knows what is best for us; and sometimes what we ask for is not what is best for us! So it may be that what you are asking for is something your family doesn't have enough money to buy, or maybe it would take too much of your time on something not good for you. So don't be sad if you don't always get what you ask for. Try to understand that it might be something you should not have.

I hope each of you have a special Christmas this year. I don't think there will be empty boxes, but I hope you will remember that some of God's best gifts are unanswered prayers.

What You Need:
- one small can labeled "I can"
- another label on the back of the can with Philippians 4:13 written out on it

I Can!

"I can do all things through Christ
which strengtheneth me."
—Philippians 4:13, KJV

I really can't ask you to guess what is in my bag without showing it to you first, so that is what I will do. Can you tell me what this is? *(A can.)* Yes, it is a can, but this is a *special* can. (Let children guess again.) This is an "I can!" What does that mean? It reminds us of all the things we can do! Tell me some of the things you can do. (Let them respond.) Is there anything you *can't* do? Can you drive your parents' car? *(No.)*

Who helps you to learn how to do new things? *(Parents, brothers, sisters, teachers.)* There is Someone else who can teach you the most important things you need to know. Can you guess who that is? *(Jesus.)*

When I turn this "I can" around, there is a verse on the back of it that comes from Philippians 4:13. It states, "I can do all things through Christ which strengtheneth me" (KJV).

That is what my "I can" stands for! You can make your own "I can" with the same things written on it and put it on your dresser to help you remember that Jesus can teach you the things you need to know from His Word, the Bible.

If there is something you are having a hard time learning, it would be good for you to write it on a small piece of paper, put it in the "I can," and say a special prayer to Jesus for help.

Eyeglasses

What You Need:
- two pairs of eyeglasses with different prescriptions

" 'For I know the plans I have for you,' declares the LORD,
'plans to prosper you and not to harm you,
plans to give you hope and a future.' "
—Jeremiah 29:11, NIV

There are two things in my bag. They look the same, but there is a difference between them. They are both worn on your face. Do you know what they are? *(Eyeglasses.)*

Have any of you boys and girls ever been to the eye doctor to have your eyes checked? The doctor showed you a chart on the wall and asked you to do something. What was that? Could you read the letters on the sign or on the screen? If you couldn't read all of the letters clearly, what did the doctor order for you to wear so that you could see better? *(Eyeglasses.)*

Are all eyeglasses the same for everyone? How are they different? They are different sizes, shapes, and colors. And the lenses are made according to the prescription. Do eyeglasses always help you to see better? Yes? No? The answer is that they only help if they are the right prescription.

I need a volunteer. (Give the volunteer one of the pairs you brought to try on.) Can you see better with this pair of eyeglasses on? *(No!)* OK, try this pair. Can you see better with the second pair? No? Why not? *(It's not the right prescription for me.)* You are right! These eyeglasses were not made for you! You can probably see better without them because you probably already have good eyesight.

Our verse today states that God knows the plans He has for you. When you are growing up, it is sometimes difficult to decide the best way to live your life. How can you make a good decision? Did you know that if you pray for God to reveal what His plans are for you, Jesus will be your eyeglasses so that you can learn about His plan for you? How does He do that? He provides you with the "eyeglasses" to see. What are the glasses that He gives? Your glasses are your Bible!

If you read your Bible and ask Jesus to help you decide the plan for your life, He will teach you through His Word to see clearly and help you live a happy life. Would you like Jesus to be your eyeglasses?

Follow

"Listen to my instruction and be wise;
do not disregard it."
—Proverbs 8:33, NIV

Today I have a piece of paper in my bag, and it has *one* very important word written on it. Let me show it to you. Can you read it? *(Follow.)* Who can tell me what the word *follow* means? (Let the children respond.)

OK, let's play a game to see if you can *follow* me. The name of the game is Simon Says. Who knows how to play Simon Says? Let me explain. If I say, "Simon says stand up," then you stand up; but if I just say, "Stand up," then you do not stand up. Do you understand the rules?

Let's try to see if you understand. "Right hand up." Did you raise your hand? Try again. "Simon says left hand up." Everyone should have their left hand up. Now you have to keep your left hand up and do whatever Simon says next. Are you ready to play the game?

(Give them some orders—some with Simon says and some not.)

Did you know that to follow Jesus, you have to follow similar instructions? If Jesus says to do something, you should *do it*. If He *doesn't* say to do it or if He says *don't* do it, then you should *not* do it. If you ask Jesus every day, He will prepare you to live with Him in heaven. The problem is the devil doesn't want you to follow Jesus. He will tell you it is OK to not follow Jesus.

Who do you want to follow—Jesus or the devil? (Let them respond.) Jesus has told us He has gone to prepare a place for us. I pray we will all meet together in heaven with Jesus.

Glue

"LORD Almighty, blessed is the one
who trusts in you."
—Psalm 84:12, NIV

What You Need:
➤ wood glue
➤ two small pieces of wood
➤ one large piece of paper—
on the floor

Who can describe what *faith* is? Hold up your hand if you have faith. When you have faith, it means you trust or believe something is true. I have something in my bag that I think will show you *what faith is* and *how* it works. Do you want to see it?

Do you think these two pieces of wood will stick together if I put glue on them? *(Yes. No.)* Let's see! I am going to glue one side of this piece of wood and stick it to this other piece of wood. Now I'll turn them over. (Pieces should fall apart.) What is the problem? *(Didn't let it dry; takes time.)* That is the way faith works. You must believe that God will answer your prayers, and then give Him time!

God knows what is best and when He should answer your prayers. The more times you use this glue to put wood together and then let it dry, the more you will believe it will hold the wood together. You learn to trust the glue. It is the same with trust in God. The more you pray and then wait until Jesus answers your prayer, the more you will trust Him.

I hope you will trust Jesus every day. I am going to place these two pieces of wood together, let them sit until church is over, and see if my faith in the glue is good. Ask me after church, and we'll see if they are stuck together.

Grapes or Raisins

"Rejoice in the Lord always.
I will say it again: Rejoice!"
—Philippians 4:4, NIV

Raise your hand if you like to eat! Who likes to eat fruit? I have a fruit in my bag that grows in a bunch. Can you guess which fruit it is? *(Grapes.)* Would you like to see them? (Take out raisins.) Don't these grapes look good? *(No!)* Why not? They are all dried up! Let me look in my bag again. (Take out grapes.) Do these look better? *(Yes!)* These are fresh and full of life!

Do you know that Christian boys and girls are sometimes like these dried-up raisins and sometimes like these full-of-life grapes. Satan doesn't like for you to be happy, and he tries to lead you away from Jesus.

Jesus told us He is the Life. He will fill us full of joy, full of happiness, and full of the life we want to live. When other boys and girls see that you are living your life like these beautiful grapes and not like these dried-up grapes (raisins), they will know that you love Jesus and that He lives in your heart.

Would you like for Jesus to help you to be happy and full of life like these grapes, or would you like for Satan to take that happiness away and "dry" you up like these raisins? If you ask Jesus every morning to fill you with His love, you will be a happy "grape."

Gravity

What You Need:
➤ one rock (not large)
➤ a small rock for each child

"Submit yourselves, then, to God.
Resist the devil, and he will flee from you."
—James 4:7, NIV
"Keep your lives free from the love of money and
be content with what you have, because God has said,
'Never will I leave you; never will I forsake you.' "
—Hebrews 13:5, NIV

In my bag today is an item that when thrown will always fall down, no matter how I throw it. The reason it always falls down is because of something called "gravity." Gravity! Who knows what *gravity* means? (Let the children respond.) Some people call it a force. It is like a big magnet.

Is there anywhere we can go to get away from gravity? *(Yes.)* There is if you get far enough away from the earth into space. Did you know that the sun has gravity? *(Yes.)* Its gravity holds all the planets in our solar system in place. The sun's gravity—or force—is stronger than the earth's gravity.

I want to tell you about two different forces. Have you ever heard someone say, "The devil made me do it"? Satan—the devil—is a strong force, and he will keep pulling you down, just like the earth's gravity holds you on the ground. He will not go away unless you tell him to go away. And even then he will keep coming back to tempt you. He is just like planet Earth's gravity. But there is another force who is stronger than Satan, just like the sun's gravity is stronger than planet Earth's gravity. Do you know who He is? Jesus! God's Son!

Do you know how to keep Jesus by your side? Jesus will never leave nor forsake you when you keep praying and keep reading what is written in His Word, the Bible. When you read your Sabbath School lessons, pray, and obey your parents and teachers, you will keep your thoughts on Jesus and He will always help you.

I have a rock in my bag for each of you. You can put the rock on your dresser to remind you that even though Satan is always trying to take your focus off of Jesus and to do wrong things, *Jesus* is stronger, just like the sun's gravity is stronger than the earth's gravity. Satan wants you to fall down, like this rock, but God's *Son* will hold you up if you just ask.

Raise your hand if you want God's Son, Jesus, to hold you up.

Greeting Cards

"For God so loved the world that he gave his one and only Son, that whoever believes in him shall not perish but have eternal life."
—John 3:16, NIV

I have several things in my bag that are the same, but each one is a little different. Everyone likes to receive them. Want to take a guess? Do you need more clues? Sometimes people get too busy and forget to send them. They are made from paper. You can buy them, or you can make them yourself. *(Greeting cards.)*

What kinds of cards can we send? *(Birthday, Christmas, Mother's Day, Father's Day, Get well.)* What about thank-you cards or thinking-of-you cards? Do we have to wait for a special day to send cards? *(No.)* We can tell our family and friends that we love them and are thinking of them even when it is not a special day.

Did you know that God has written "cards" for us to read that will cheer us up when we are sad or sick and "notes" to give us encouragement when we need help? He has also told us how much He loves us. Do you know where we can read His notes? *(The Bible.)*

Do we have to wait for special days or for the Sabbath to read His notes to us? *(No.)* He has given us this Book to read every day; and when you do that, you will learn what He has said about how much He loves us and how He wants us to live so that we can be happy.

You can also read the note that says He is coming back to take all of His children, both big and small, to heaven. Raise your hand if you want Him to take *you* to heaven. I pray we will see one another there!

Hair Dryer

What You Need:
- one hair dryer
- one extension cord (if needed)
- one pinwheel

"But the Advocate, the Holy Spirit, whom the Father will send in my name, will teach you all things and will remind you of everything I have said to you."
—John 14:26, NIV

What I have in my bag is probably something that most of you have in your home. Let me give you a clue. Sometimes it is hot, and sometimes it is not. It is not very big. You hold it in your hand, and it blows air. *(Hair dryer.)* What do you have to do to make it work? Can it do anything by itself? *(No.)* It must be connected to electricity, so you have to plug it in—just like we have to be plugged in to God to do what is right.

OK, so let's plug it into the electric outlet. Does it work now? *(No.)* Why not? *(You have to turn it on.)* I guess that is like having a Bible in your house but not reading and studying it. OK, I will turn it on but will set it for cool air, not hot. I need someone to help me. Hold your hand in front of the dryer. Do you feel anything? *(Yes, wind or air.)* I don't see the wind! Are you sure you feel it? *(Yes.)* The wind is invisible, but you can feel it!

I have something else in my bag. (Show the children the pinwheel.) Do you know what this is? *(Pinwheel.)* Let's put it in front of the hair dryer and see what happens. Can you see the wind now? *(No.)* But you can see the effect of the wind, can't you? When the wind blows outside, can you see it? *(No.)* But you can see the effect.

There is something interesting about the word *wind*. Did you know the original name for the Holy Spirit was *Wind*? In the old Hebrew language, the word *wind* meant "Holy Spirit."

When Jesus went back to heaven after His resurrection, He sent the Holy Spirit to be with us. The Holy Spirit is who reminds us of the good things we should do.

Can we see the Holy Spirit? *(No.)* He is like the *wind*. We can only hear and feel the effects of His guidance by listening to our conscience. Do you think your friends and parents can see the Holy Spirit in the way you act? *(Yes.)* If you talk or act unkindly, do you think others will know that you love Jesus? *(No.)* We need to pray every day that the Holy Spirit (the Wind) will affect our actions, just like the pinwheel is turned by the wind from the hair dryer.

What You Need:
- one simple children's puzzle (disassembled and missing one piece) in a ziplock bag
- the missing piece in another ziplock bag
- one flat surface to assemble the puzzle

Heaven's Puzzle

"My Father's house has many rooms; if that were not so, would I have told you that I am going there to prepare a place for you?"
—John 14:2, NIV

I want to talk about heaven today! How many of you boys and girls want to go to heaven?

I have something in my bag that has several pieces to it. Sometimes there are just a few pieces, and sometimes there are a lot of pieces. Can you guess what it is? Need more clues? Each piece is different, but they all fit together to make the whole. *(A puzzle.)*

Let's put it together to see what it looks like. (Let the children help.) What is this a picture of? Is there anything wrong with the puzzle? Yes, a piece is missing. Let me see if I can find it in my bag. Here it is! Now the puzzle is complete.

Let's pretend this puzzle is heaven and that each piece is one of you boys and girls. Is each of you different? *(Yes.)* Look at one another. Do you all look the same? *(No.)* Just like each piece of the puzzle is different, each one of you is different. Is it all right that you are not all alike? *(Yes.)* What would it be like if everyone was the same? Not so interesting? Even though each of you has your own features and talents, you have things in common. You all have ears, eyes, a nose, arms and legs, and so on.

You raised your hands that you want to go to heaven. What would it be like to go there and find out that one of you were missing? Heaven would not be complete! Is the puzzle pretty with one piece missing? *(No.)* There is a small hole where the missing piece fits. Jesus wants each one of you to be a piece of heaven so that you will make the picture complete.

Shall we ask Jesus to help you to be a piece of heaven every day? (Pray.)

Helpers

"You study the Scriptures diligently because you think
that in them you have eternal life.
These are the very Scriptures that testify about me."
—John 5:39, NIV

What You Need:
- three pieces of wood
- one hammer
- one saw
- one screwdriver
- one nail
- one screw
- one Bible
- one Sabbath School quarterly
- four books or magazines

Whew, my bag is heavy! I have many show-and-tell things today.

Have any of you ever had to do something you couldn't do by yourself, something you needed help with? *(Yes.)* I need three helpers to assist me with some of the things in my bag—things I cannot do by myself. (Choose three helpers.) Let's see what we have here—three pieces of wood. What I need is for you three to hold one piece of wood each. Now that you are holding the wood, do you need a helper? *(No.)* Let's see what else I have in my bag: a hammer, a saw, and a screwdriver. I need three more volunteers to hold these tools. (Choose three more volunteers.) Do any of you need help yet? *(No.)*

Now I need the hammer to cut one of the pieces of wood. (Put the two children with those items together.) Next I need the screwdriver to hammer the nail into the next piece of wood. (Put the two children together and give the nail to the child with the screwdriver.) Now we need the saw to drive the screw into the last piece of wood. (Put the two children together and give the screw to the child with the saw.) Are you helping one another? *(No.)* Is there something wrong? You don't have the right tools for what I asked you to do? Who should help whom? (Let the children choose the child who has the tool to match the job. Now have the children put the wood and tools down.)

Let me ask you a question. What tools do you need to help you follow Jesus and to live the life of a Christian?

I have something else in my bag that might be helpful to you. Books and magazines! What do you think—do these look like they would be good things for you to read? Which ones will help you to know Jesus? *(The Bible and the Sabbath School quarterly.)* You are right! What about these other ones? All the other books and magazines are good to read, but they don't talk about Jesus. The Bible and the Sabbath School quarterly will help you to know Jesus better, just like having the right tool is necessary for your helper to do the job with the wood.

Thank you for your help! Use the "Jesus tools" every day so that you will know how He wants you to live.

Hickory Nut

"Therefore put on the full armor of God, so that when the day of evil comes, you may be able to stand your ground, and after you have done everything, to stand."

—Ephesians 6:13, NIV

Have any of you boys and girls ever seen a suit of armor? Can you tell me what it does? *(Yes.)* It protects you.

I have one in my bag! Would you like to see it? (Bring out the nut.) Is this what you thought it would look like? *(No.)* You were thinking of a heavy, metal suit of armor, weren't you? My bag is definitely not big enough for that kind of armor.

But *is* this a "suit of armor"? *(Yes.)* It has various parts to it that protect the nut inside so that it can grow until it is mature (ripe). Without the armor, the nut would be eaten by bugs or burnt by the sun. Let's look at the parts of this nut. (Crack the nut, and show the shell, the skin, and the nut.)

Did you know that God gives each one of you boys and girls a suit of armor? There are several places in the Bible that explain this to us. Ephesians 6:13 states, "Put on the full armor of God" (NIV), so when Satan tries to get you to do wrong, you will be covered by God's protection.

Would this armor over the nut be any good if it only covered one-half of the nut? *(No.)* That is why God tells us to put on every piece of armor. The pieces He puts in His armor are faith, hope, and love. This afternoon ask your parents to help you find the verses that tell about the whole armor of God. He wants you to be protected from Satan so that you will be ready to go to heaven when Jesus comes.

Raise your hand if you want to be safely within the armor of God.

Honor and Obey

"Show proper respect to everyone, love the family of believers,
fear God, honor the emperor."
—1 Peter 2:17, NIV

What You Need:
► one photo of the president
► one photo of a police officer

have a couple of pictures of people in my bag. Can you tell me who this is? (Show photo of the president.) Who is this? *(The president.)* What is he the president of? *(The United States.)*

When the president of the United States enters a room, is there something special that people do? *(Stand up!)* Have you ever seen the president on TV? Have you seen what else people do, besides stand, when he enters the room? *(They clap.)* Clapping is a way of showing honor to the president. Here is another picture of a person. What do we call a person who wears a uniform like this? *(A police officer.)* When a police officer talks to you, do you say, "Yes, sir," or "No, ma'am"? Do we need to show respect to a police officer when he or she speaks to us? *(Yes.)*

Can you tell me which of the Ten Commandments tells us to honor the president of the United States or a police officer? None of the commandments do. But there is a Bible verse: Romans 13:1, 2 says that we should be respectful to the governing authorities.

But who does the fifth commandment tell us to honor and obey? *(Your father and mother.)* "Honor your father and your mother, so that you may live long in the land the LORD your God is giving you" (Exodus 20:12, NIV).

Do each of you always do what your parents ask you to do, right away and with a happy smile on your face? Jesus wants us to honor our parents. If you have sinned against your parents, you can still ask Jesus to forgive you, and He will. Who else should you ask to forgive you? *(Yes, your parents.)* Ask Jesus to help you not to make that mistake again.

Raise your hand if you want to obey the fifth commandment and to honor your parents.

What you Need:
▸ one jar of hot water
▸ one jar of cold water

Hot and Cold Water

"I know your deeds, that you are neither cold nor hot.
I wish you were either one or the other!"
—Revelation 3:15, NIV

I have two things in my bag that look the same, but there is something different about each one. The jars look the same, and the liquids inside looks the same; but they aren't the same. Want to make a guess? (Show the jars.) I need a helper to feel the outside of the jars. How are they different? *(One is hot, and one is cold.)*

Have you ever wanted a cold drink of water but could only find hot water to drink? It wasn't very good, was it? You can put some flavoring (such as powdered chocolate) in the hot water to make it taste better; but hot water, by itself, isn't very good. Have you ever taken a shower and had the hot water run out before you finished? That, for sure, is not fun! All of a sudden your water turns cold, and you have to hurry to get done. It's especially not fun when you have shampoo in your hair at the time the hot water runs out.

Did you know that each one of us is somewhat like this water? I look at you, and you all look somewhat the same on the outside. You all have arms and legs, eyes, ears, a mouth, a nose, and so on. But I cannot know what you are like on the inside—if you are connected to Jesus or not (hot or cold, good or bad). Only Jesus knows what is in your hearts. He wants us to be *hot* when it comes to loving Him. If we neglect talking to Him every day and reading what the Bible says, our love for Jesus will grow cold.

When it is cold outside, what do you do to get warm? *(Put on a sweater or a coat.)* What can you do to stay *hot* with Jesus? Read your Bible and pray! I hope you will remember to stay *hot* with Jesus.

I Love Jesus—Backward

"Remember the Sabbath day by keeping it holy."
—Exodus 20:8, NIV

What You Need:
▸ one sign with the phrase *I love Jesus* written backward
▸ one mirror (as large as will fit in your bag)
▸ Calendar

I made a sign! It's in my bag. Would you like to see it? Can anyone read it? (If someone guesses right away, ask if it was hard to read.) If you look at the sign in the mirror, can you read it then? *(I love Jesus.)* Is there something wrong with the way I wrote it? *(It is backward.)*

Raise your hand if you have seen an ambulance. Did you notice that on the front of the ambulance, the word *ambulance* was written backward? Do you know why? It is so that when the driver of the car in front of the ambulance looks in the rearview mirror, he or she will see the word written properly. Then the driver knows to get out of the way, so the ambulance can pass.

When a shirt you are wearing has a word printed on it, you will see the word backward when you look down on it, but the person coming toward you will see it the way it should be.

So should our lives be backward? *(No!)* We should live our lives so that people will know we are following Jesus and not Satan. When people do things that make Satan happy, they make Jesus sad, and that is a sign that a change is needed.

Some people might think you are backward today because you are in church on Saturday, the Sabbath, and not Sunday. Do you know why they think that is backward? It's because most people think Sunday is the day we should go to church. But the Bible states, "Remember the sabbath day, to keep it holy. Six days shalt thou labour, and do all thy work: but the seventh day is the sabbath of the LORD thy God" (Exodus 20:8–10, KJV). (Show a calendar. Have someone number off the days of the week.)

The Sabbath is like a sign to remind us of God and Creation. If we are following the Sabbath sign, people will wonder why, and we can tell them that is because we are following what Jesus asked us to do. We don't want to be backward. We want to go forward with Jesus as our Guide.

Raise your hand if you want to go to heaven and be with Jesus.

What You Need:
▸ one iPad or tablet

iPad or Tablet

"All Scripture is God-breathed and is useful for teaching, rebuking, correcting and training in righteousness."
—2 Timothy 3:16, NIV

Who can tell me what an iPad is? Do any of you have one? What about a tablet? Is it the same as an iPad? Yes, it is the same. It is also different, sort of like how boys and girls are the same with eyes, ears, legs, and hands, but they are different in many other ways.

Do you know how to use an iPad or a tablet? What do you have to do first? *(Turn it on.)* No, something else comes first. It must be plugged in and charged! After it is charged, then can you turn it on? *(Yes.)* (Turn it on.) OK. What comes next? Sometimes there is a special password or code you have to enter so that you can use it. (Put in the code.) Then what happens? The main screen comes on. What is on the screen? Many different things known as "apps," a short word for *applications.* From here, you can select a game, a picture, a book, or lots of other things. Do some of these things take a lot of your time? *(Yes.)*

Did you know your Bible can be one of the apps you can choose? Do you take time to read your Bible on your iPad or tablet? Of course, you don't need an iPad or tablet to read your Bible, do you? But do you take time to read *your* Bible?

Let's compare how an iPad or tablet is like each one of you. What is the first thing you do every day? *(Get up, eat?)* Well, you first have to sleep, don't you? OK, so after you sleep, *then* you get up. You eat sometime soon afterward, right? Food helps to charge your body with energy. Without a good breakfast, your body isn't really ready for the day.

What next? Can you guess what should be next to start your day, an important "password" that will help you to have a good day? Something you should do every morning (and many other times throughout your day). *(Pray.)* Yes, prayer is important because if you start your day with Jesus, whatever happens, He will remind you that He wants to help you to have a good day. Jesus can teach you wherever you are. You can learn by being outside around flowers, birds, trees, stars, and lots of other things.

I hope you will take time to learn about Jesus and how He loves you and me. He came to this earth to die and take away our sins just so He can take us to live with Him in heaven forever.

Kites

What You Need:
- one kite
- string
- one kite tail

"Teach me to do your will, for you are my God; may your good Spirit lead me on level ground."
—Psalm 143:10, NIV

Have any of you ever flown a kite? (Let the children respond.) Was it fun? What color was it? Did it have a picture on it? Flying a kite is tricky but a lot of fun. If you haven't ever flown one, maybe your parents will buy one for you and show you how to fly it.

What do you need to have to fly a kite? A kite, string, a tail, and *wind*. Wind is very important. All four things are necessary! The last time I took my kite out it was very windy, so I thought it would be easy to fly it. It went straight up as fast as I could let the string out, and then it suddenly went straight down and crashed on the ground. I was so happy that it didn't break! I had to keep adding more tail to the kite to keep it balanced. When I finally got enough tail, it was really fun to fly. Do you think it was my holding the string that made the kite fly? *(No.)* It was the wind. When the wind blew less, the kite started to come down; and when it blew harder, the kite went back up. The kite did what the wind caused it to do. I had no control over the wind.

Do you ever do what *you* want to do instead of what your parents want you to do? Sometimes Satan tempts us to make bad choices; and when we listen to him, the result is just like what happens to the kite when there is not enough wind. We fall and crash! If we pull hard on the string of a kite, we can avoid letting it crash. If we ask Jesus to help us make good choices, He will keep us from crashing.

One time when the wind was blowing hard, the string holding my kite broke. What do you think happened to my kite? It went flying away from me, going up and down and in circles until it crashed on the ground. I thought I had lost it. I had to walk a long way to another field, but I was happy to eventually find it.

Next time you fly a kite or see someone else flying a kite, remember how important it is to allow Jesus to guide you like the wind guides the kite. Jesus needs to be in control of your life. God gave your parents to you to help you make good choices.

What You Need:

▸ knives
▸ forks
▸ spoons
▸ one tray to fit them into

Knife, Fork, and Spoon Tray

"Each of you should use whatever gift you have received to serve others, as faithful stewards of God's grace in its various forms."
—1 Peter 4:10, NIV

There are some things in my bag that need to be put back where they belong. They each look different, but they are all used to serve the same purpose. Any guesses? (Let the children respond, then show them the utensils.) *(A knife, a fork, and a spoon.)* Do they all look the same? *(No.)* They are all different. What makes them the same? Do you use all of them to help you eat? *(Yes.)* Can you eat soup with a fork? *(No.)* Can you eat soup with a knife? *(No.)* What do you need to eat soup? (Let them respond.) Yes, a spoon works best. I have a tray that is specially made to hold knives, forks, and spoons. As you can see, there are special places for each item. They are different sizes to match the sizes of the utensils.

The tray is somewhat like our church. Each one of us is different, but we all fit into the church. I'd like all of you boys to stand. Let's see if you are different or the same. *Hmm.* Not all the same. OK, sit down. Now all of you girls stand up. *Hmm.* Not all the same! Everyone who is four years old, stand up. Do you all have the same birthday? *(No.)* Stand up if you have blond hair. Is everyone the same? *(No.)* One more question. If you love Jesus, stand up. This is one way that everybody is the same! You all love Jesus. There is another thing that makes you all the same. It is the way Jesus loves you. He loves every one of you the same, and He wants you to live in heaven with Him.

Do you want to fit into heaven just like the silverware fits in the tray—all different, but all the same in your love for Jesus? Although we look different and have different talents, we are the same in that we all love Jesus and want to use our special gifts to fit the place He has prepared for us. I hope you plan to live in heaven with your family and friends and, best of all, with Jesus.

Knife, Fork, and Spoon

"Therefore go and make disciples of all nations, baptizing them
in the name of the Father and of the Son and of the Holy Spirit."
—Matthew 28:19, NIV

What You Need:
- knife
- fork
- spoon
- set of plastic utensils for each child

I have three things in my bag that go together. They are a set. Need some clues? Each one is different, but together they make one. Each one has its special job, but together they are a team—a set. You use them when you eat. Now do you know? *(Silverware.)* They are a knife, a fork, and a spoon. How do they work together? Does each have a special job? Have you ever tried to eat soup with a fork or eat peas with a knife?

Can you think of three beings in the Bible who are different but who each have a specific purpose—and who together are one? God the Father; His Son, Jesus; and the Holy Spirit! God the Father is in heaven. He sent His Son, Jesus, to earth to show us how to live and follow the Ten Commandments. And when Jesus went back to heaven, He sent the Holy Spirit to come into our hearts and minds to help us know what is right and wrong. He is our teacher, our comforter, and our conscience.

Do you believe it would be a good idea to think of the gift we have in the help of God the Father; His Son, Jesus; and the Holy Spirit when you pick up your silverware to eat? You can thank Them, all three of Them, who have special purposes but who all together are one *God*? I hope this story will help you to remember to thank all three—the Father; the Son, Jesus; and the Holy Spirit every time you eat.

I have a set of plastic silverware for each of you to help you remember this story.

Free Gift: Knife, Fork, and Spoon (Follow-Up)

"For it is by grace you have been saved, through faith— and this is not from yourselves, it is the gift of God."
—Ephesians 2:8, NIV

Last week I gave you something. Do you remember what it was? Silverware! Do you remember what it represented? *(God the Father; His Son, Jesus; and the Holy Spirit.)* Very good! Did any of you boys and girls save the silverware to help you remember to thank all three of Them when you prayed at mealtimes?

How much did you pay for the silverware? Nothing. It was free! It was free to you because I paid the price for it and was glad to do that for you!

When you pray to Jesus for forgiveness of your sins, how much do you have to pay Him? Nothing! It is a free gift from Jesus. Jesus paid the price for your sins and for mine. Do you know how He paid the price? He died on the cross and rose from the dead to take our sins away so that they would never be seen again. He died so that each one of us can go to heaven to live with Him forever.

How much do we have to pay to have our sins forgiven? Nothing! All we have to do is *ask* Jesus and believe that He has taken them away forever!

Labels

"By this everyone will know that you
are my disciples, if you love one another."
—John 13:35, NIV

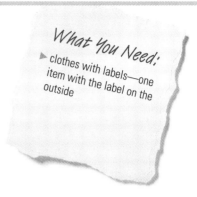

What You Need:
➤ clothes with labels—one
item with the label on the
outside

have several things in my bag, and each has something attached that reveals information about it. When I was a young boy, these attached things were always sewn to the inside. Now, many times they are on the outside. Does anyone want to guess? They are *labels*! Does anyone know what information can be found on a label? (Let the children respond.) Some labels give instructions on how to take care of the item, such as "machine wash"; "wool, dry clean only"; or "hand wash in cold water." Also, the clothing will probably have a label, which shows the size of the item as well as where it was made.

Sometimes people label other people. Not that they actually sew a label on them—not in *that* way! But sometimes we label a person by saying things that may not be true—things like "he doesn't like me," "she is always so mean," "she is too skinny," "he thinks he is better than everyone," or "she always wears ugly clothes." Have you ever labeled someone? Sometimes the labels we put on others are not very nice and make them sad.

There is one label that is a good kind of label; a good name would be another way to say it. When people look at you, it would be a nice label if they were to say, "He (she) is a Christian." Wherever we go, it would be good if people recognized that we love Jesus. The things we say and the way we act give clues as to whether or not we are Christians. If we say we are Christians but talk bad about others, some might think all Christians are like that and would never decide to be a Christian. We need to ask Jesus to help us to be kind and loving. Remember to think, *What would Jesus do?*

When Jesus lived on this earth, He was given several labels or names. Can you tell me some of them? (Let them respond.) God, Healer, Teacher, Prophet, Wonderful, and Counselor are a few.

If we want to go to heaven, we'll need to have a good label. Remember that you are wearing a label that says, "I am a Seventh-day Adventist Christian" boy or girl. If you have the Christian label, that means you want to be like Christ. *Christian* means "Christlike." Do you wear a good label, one you can be proud to wear?

Light

"While I am in the world,
I am the light of the world."
—John 9:5, NIV

I have something in my bag that helps people see in the dark. Can you guess what it is? *(Flashlight.)* Let's pretend that it is dark in the church. Now would this flashlight be helpful? (Don't turn it on.) *(No.)* Why not? *(Because it is not on!)* You are correct! Let's try something. I want all of you to shut your eyes tight—no peeking. Can you tell me if the light is on or off? *(No.)* Why can't you tell me? *(Because our eyes are closed!)* That's right! The only way you can see the light is to open your eyes.

Did you know that when Jesus lived on this earth, He told everyone that He is the "Light of the world"? What must you do to see the light of Jesus? Open your eyes. How do we open our eyes to see Jesus? We read about Him in the Bible. It tells us what Jesus is like. It shows us how much He loves us by the things He made for us to enjoy—things we find in nature, such as flowers, trees, birds, and all the other things Jesus made for us to see. He has given us so many beautiful things to enjoy, and His Word, the Bible, tells us how much He loves you and me. That way we know He is wonderful.

Raise your hand if you want to be able to see Jesus better and to be ready when He comes to take you to heaven. All of you! I am so glad you are anxious to see Him.

Remember that this flashlight won't help you see if your eyes are closed. I pray that each one of you will open your eyes and learn the things He wants you to know about Him and read about Him every day. I want to see each one of you boys and girls in heaven.

Locks

What You Need:
➤ one key lock
➤ one combination lock
➤ one group of keys
➤ one list of numbers

"Ask and it will be given to you; seek and you will find;
knock and the door will be opened to you."
—Matthew 7:7, NIV

I have two things in my bag that serve the same purpose, but they are different. Do you need some clues? Sometimes they are open and sometimes not. Need more clues? Sometimes you need a key, but sometimes you need to know numbers. Sometimes they can keep things in, and sometimes they can keep things out. Now can you guess? *(Locks.)*

I have two kinds of locks. Is there a difference? What is it? One is a combination lock, and it is opened by turning the dial back and forth with specific numbers. Do you think it matters which way you turn the dial and which numbers you use? *(Yes.)* (I will tell you more about that in another story.) The other is a key lock and is opened with a key. Does it matter what key we use? *(Yes.)* If you don't use the correct key, the lock will still be locked.

As you grow older, you will need many different keys. You'll probably need a house key, a locker key at school, a car key, and an office key at work.

There is another key that everyone needs. This key is spoken about in the Bible, and it opens your connection with Jesus. Can you guess what it is? *(Prayer!)* If we pray to Jesus every day, He will open the right doors so that we will do what He knows is best for us. Keeping in touch with Him every day will keep us happy no matter what happens, because we know we can trust Him. He can help us choose good friends, good things to read, good games to play, good things to watch, good things to eat—all the choices we make every day.

You will learn that Jesus can and will help you in everything you do all day long because He is your friend. Raise your hand if you want Jesus to protect you by teaching you to use the key to His prayer lock of safety.

Long and Short

"For God so loved the world that he gave his one and only Son, that whoever believes in him shall not perish but have eternal life."
—John 3:16, NIV

have several of something in my bag. Some of you use one almost every day. Sometimes they are long, and sometimes they are short. Want to make a guess? I'll give you another clue. They come in different colors, but they all have two things in common—two things that are the same. Do you give up? One more clue first. Those of you who use one do so while at school. Now do you know? Pencils! (Bring out the loose one.) Do you want to see the rest of them? What are the two things that make them all the same? *(They all have lead and erasers!)*

Do you think all these pencils are the same length? Can you tell me which one is the shortest and which one is the longest? I need helpers to choose some pencils. What makes you think the one you picked is the longest or shortest? (Let the child respond.) *(The eraser has or hasn't been used.)* Let's see! (Remove the chosen pencils one by one. When each child has each given their reason, show the pencils they have chosen.) Now do you think you have picked the shortest and the longest? (Now uncover the remaining ones to see if they were correct.)

Let's compare you boys and girls with pencils. Do you know why I think you are like pencils? Because you all are different sizes, different colors, and dressed differently. Is there anything that is the same for all of you? *(Body parts.)* Yes, that is correct, but each part is different from someone else's. The same parts may be different shapes, sizes, or colors.

What do you think might be the same for all of you? You *all* are God's children! God *loves* each of you the same! Even though you may be older and have an arm that is bigger than your friend's arm, have blond hair compared to brown hair, or have whatever difference you may have, the thing you all have in common is *God's* love. You also have Jesus' love and the love of the Holy Spirit. All three want you to be in heaven.

I want all of you to have one of these pencils to remember that no matter if you are short or tall, a boy, or a girl, you are all God's children, and He loves each one of you the same!

Lots of Legs

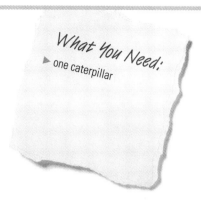

What You Need:
► one caterpillar

"God is with us; he is our leader."
—2 Chronicles 13:12, NIV

How many of you have played the game follow-the-leader? It's a simple game to play. Someone is chosen to be the leader, and everyone else has to go where the leader goes and do what the leader does. Do you think that would be fun? If you haven't played before, ask your parents to play it with you sometime.

I have something in my bag today that likes to play follow-the-leader. Would you like to see it? *(It's a caterpillar.)* Can you see that it has lots of legs? What would happen if the legs in the middle decided they wanted to go in another direction, instead of following the leader? What if the last legs decided to meet the front legs and go in another direction? Is it important that there is only *one* leader? *(Yes.)* What if this caterpillar had two leaders. Would that cause some confusion for the other legs? Who would the rest of the legs follow?

Did you know that a long time ago there was war in heaven because one of the angels decided he wanted to be the leader? Do you know who started the war? *(The devil, Satan.)* He wanted to be the leader of Jesus and everyone else. He tried to get all of the angels to follow him instead of Jesus. Do you know what happened? God made Satan leave heaven. Some of the angels chose to follow Satan, and they had to leave as well. What a sad day for God. He didn't want that to happen. He didn't want Eve to listen to Satan either, because her choice meant sin had come to this earth. Satan likes to tempt you and me to do wrong things and to stop following Jesus.

If we were like the legs of the caterpillar and we did wrong things and tried to go in a different direction from the leader, it would make Jesus sad. We each have to decide to follow the leader, Jesus. As long as we follow Jesus, there will be no confusion, because He will lead us up to heaven.

I hope each one of you will start each morning by asking Jesus to be your Leader, and I hope you will follow Him all day long.

What You Need:

▶ one small wooden box— big enough for a penny to slide from one side to the other and become hidden

Magic Box

"My eyes are on all their ways; they are not hidden from me, nor is their sin concealed from my eyes."
—Jeremiah 16:17, NIV

Who has seen someone do a magic trick? I have a magic box in my bag that I want to show you. Isn't it a pretty wooden box? Let's see what is in it. It's a penny! (Remove the penny.) Do you think this penny is real? *(Yes.)* Would you like to know what makes this a magic penny box? Let's put the penny back in the box. (Show everyone that it is there, and then make it disappear.) Would you like to see the penny again? It's gone! Where did it go? How many of you think the penny is really gone? Let me shake the box and see if it is still there. Did you hear it? *(Yes.)* It is hidden inside! I think I can make it appear again. Do you want to see it?

Let's compare this penny and this box with you boys and girls. This penny is like sin, and the box is like each one of us. Sometimes when we sin, we do it in front of others, and everyone around us can see or hear what we did wrong. Like if in front of the whole class, you were to tell someone at school he or she was dumb. But sometimes we think we can hide our sin when no one is around to see—like taking a cookie from a cookie jar that we aren't supposed to take from without permission from our parents.

You need to remember that when we try to hide our sin, it is still inside us, just like when this penny is hiding in the box where we can't see it. We can never hide a sin from God because He sees everything that we think we are hiding. We can't hide sin from Him. The best decision to make is to not sin; then we don't have to worry. But if you do sin and you are sorry for it, remember that you can always ask God to forgive that sin, and He will.

We all want to go to heaven to live with Jesus. So when you make a mistake and ask Him to forgive you, also ask Him to help you to not sin anymore. He will do that!

Magnet

"I keep my eyes always on the LORD.
With him at my right hand, I will not be shaken."
—Psalm 16:8, NIV

What You Need:
➤ one strong magnet
➤ one small piece of wood
➤ one penny
➤ one heavy piece of steel

I have something in my bag that will draw something else to it if it is made with some of the same thing. Confused? I'll give you a clue. It is metal and is _____ shaped. Can you guess? (Show the magnet.) This is a strong magnet. Let's see how strong it is. (Hold up the small piece of wood.) Will the magnet pick up this piece of wood? (Try it.) *Hmm.* Let's see if it will pick up this little penny. (Try it.) *Hmm.* I thought it would pick up metal. Let's try this steel _____. It worked! I guess the magnet only picks up certain kinds of metal, like this steel. Let me hold it up again to see how strong it is. (Let the magnet draw something from a distance.) Look at that! Did you think this magnet would be that strong? (Let the children respond.)

So you have to know what is true and what is not true about this magnet. It isn't true that it will pick up anything that is metal, right? It has to be something that is made of steel, just like the magnet is made from steel. You need to learn that some things you will hear and see as you grow up will not always be true, and you need to ask Jesus to help you know the difference between what is true and what is false.

I want to show you something else about this magnet. (Get a helper from the congregation.) If Mr. _____ holds his keys (Do not use keys with an electric door opener attached!) near the magnet, will the magnet hold both this steel _____ and the keys? *(Yes.)* What if we put them at the end of _____? *(No.)* Why? The strength of the magnet gets weaker as you get farther away from the source of power!

Who can you think of that is like this magnet? Strong, powerful, who draws you to Him when you seek His help. Do you know who that is? Jesus! He wants you to be close to Him, just like this magnet will hold to this steel _____. The problem is when you walk away from Jesus you will no longer have His power to keep you from problems—unless you move closer to Him again and ask Him for His power. Does the power of Jesus quit? *(No.)* His power is always strong. It is up to you and me to stay close to the power of Jesus, and He will hold us firm.

Jesus will never quit reaching out to you. He loves you so much that He left heaven to become a baby and to live a perfect life for our example. He died to take all our sins away and is now in heaven preparing to come and take you and me to live with Him. Raise your hand if you want to stay close to Jesus to receive His power every day.

Match

"A gentle answer turns away wrath,
but a harsh word stirs up anger."
—Proverbs 15:1, NIV

I have something in my bag that is very useful but can also be very destructive. Sometimes it is hot, and sometimes not. Need a clue? It can provide some light. *(Match.)*

Do you know why I said it is sometimes useful but sometimes destructive? It is good when a match is used to make heat to keep us warm. But if it is used to start a fire that is not wanted, then it is bad. When does a match get hot? It only gets hot when you light it. What do you have to do to light it? Rub it against something. Does it matter what we use to light it? *(Yes.)* We rub only the rough part on the matchbox. (Strike the box, and light the match.)

When there is a storm and the electricity goes off, it is good to have a match to light a candle that will give off light. Can you think of a time when a match would be used to light something special for you to blow out? What about the candles on your birthday cake?

One little burning match can start a huge fire in a forest when the weeds are dry. That is not a good thing, is it?

Let's compare ourselves with this match. Most of the time we are obedient, but sometimes we make wrong decisions and sin. What happens when you rub up against something rough, like getting mad at your friend? Do you get *hot?* Have you ever been mad—so mad your face turned red? Every day Satan does his best to make us disobedient and to make us hot!

We have to ask Jesus to help us stay cool when Satan tries to make us hot. If you are tempted to do something wrong when you get mad, *stop!* A simple prayer to Jesus will remind you to calm down. Jesus will help you to make a good decision to not say or do something that you shouldn't. If you don't listen to Jesus and you decide to do the wrong thing anyway, you will feel sad and sorry for it. So remember that when you admit you were wrong and ask Jesus to forgive you, He will do that.

I'm giving you a burnt match that you can keep by your bedside to remind you not to get hot and burn up. All you have to do is ask Jesus for help.

Matryoshka Doll

What You Need:
▶ one matryoshka doll

"But the Lord said to Samuel, 'Do not consider his appearance or his height, for I have rejected him. The Lord does not look at the things people look at. People look at the outward appearance, but the Lord looks at the heart.' "
—1 Samuel 16:7, NIV

What I have in my bag today is something very special. It is something made in a faraway country known as Russia. Would you like to see it? It is called a matryoshka doll. It is hand-painted, which means that the artist painted the features on the doll by hand using his or her artistic talent. I think it is pretty. Do you agree?

There is a saying that some of you may have heard that goes like this: "Beauty is only skin deep." Do you know what that means? It means that you may look pretty on the outside, but that the way you are on the inside, your talk and your actions, may not be so pretty.

Let me show you something about this matryoshka doll. You already agreed that the doll is pretty, right? Let's look on the inside! Another pretty doll! Inside that one is another one. There are several inside each other, and all of them are pretty. The inside dolls are as pretty as the outside dolls.

Does Jesus just look on the outside? *(No.)* It isn't as important to Him what we look like on the outside as what our characters are like on the inside. Boys and girls with good characters are children who are honest, loving, and kind on the inside. That's the type of "pretty" that Jesus loves.

How can we have pretty characters? By becoming like Jesus. If we pray to Him every day and ask Him to help us with the way we talk and the way we act, we will become like Him. So if one of your friends asks or tempts you to do something that is not "pretty," you can send up a quick prayer to Jesus. He will help you say, "No, that isn't the way Jesus wants me to be." A *real* friend will not ask you to do wrong things, and Jesus will help you to choose good friends.

Let's look at the matryoshka doll again! She is pretty on the inside and the outside, just as Jesus wants us to be.

What You Need:
▸ one ear of corn (Count the kernels before telling the story.)

Corn Miracles

"Follow my example, as I follow the example of Christ."
—1 Corinthians 11:1, NIV

Raise your hand if you believe in miracles. A *miracle* is "an outstanding event considered to be the work of Divine intervention." Wow, that's a lot of big words. A *miracle* is a wonderful, marvelous mystery. One of my friends was told by his doctor that he had a problem that could not be fixed and that he would die soon. But he didn't die. Not only that, but when another X-ray was taken of his problem, the doctor said the problem was no longer there. "It's a miracle," he said.

I have a miracle in my bag! Would you like to see it? What is this? *(An ear of corn.)*
Would you like to know why this ear of corn is a miracle? Have any of you boys and girls ever planted corn in a garden? Do you know what a kernel of corn is? (Show the children.) Just this one little piece! Do you know how many kernels of corn you have to plant to make one ear? *(One.)* Would someone like to guess how many kernels of corn are on this ear? (Mine had ___.) Who knows how many ears grow on one plant? *(One to two.)* Just think—one kernel planted in the ground can make (___) kernels. Isn't that a wonderful miracle?

Did you know that God wants each of us to be like this little kernel of corn? He wants us to tell others about Jesus and His love because, when we do, the number of people who follow Him will multiply and multiply. *Multiply* means to increase greatly in number.

How do you think you can show others what Jesus is like? The best way is to act like Jesus. How do you know how He acts? By reading about Him in the Bible, by praying, by studying your Sabbath School lesson, by reading about how others have led people to Jesus, and by obeying your parents and teachers.

Raise your hand if you want to multiply the number of people who follow Jesus from watching your example of what it is to be like Him, just like one kernel of corn is multiplied when it is planted in the ground. I hope and pray you will multiply also.

Miracles in Flowers

What You Need:
- flowers
- seeds

"I can do all this through him
who gives me strength."
—Philippians 4:13, NIV

Who can explain the meaning of a miracle? It is a little hard to describe, isn't it? I heard a story about a girl who was very sick, so sick the doctor told her mother that there was no way he could make her better. He thought she would die that night. This mother loved Jesus very much, so during the night, she wiped the fevered sweat off her little girl's face and sang the girl's favorite Jesus songs as she prayed for her little girl to live. In the morning, the daughter's fever was gone, and she was sitting on the side of her bed asking for breakfast. When the doctor came in, he said, "It's a miracle. Jesus has healed her." Has anyone here ever seen a miracle?

I have a miracle in my bag! Would you like to see it? What is this? (*Flower.*) Do you know why I say this flower is a miracle? Because it changes from a dried-up seed (Show the children some flower seeds.) to this beautiful flower.

What does the seed need to grow into a flower? (Let the children respond.) (*Dirt, water, sunshine.*) Very good. That's right!

Let's compare this flower with you boys and girls. Do you need some of the same things this flower needs to grow? (Let them guess.) You need water, food, and sunshine in order to grow, just like the flower needs those things.

There are other things you need to know to help you grow: the love of Jesus and your parents. Jesus knows just what kind of flower you are and will show you how to grow and be beautiful. When you pray and ask Jesus to help you grow, He will guide you to the very job you will do best—maybe a teacher, a nurse, a mother, a painter, a lawyer, a father, a builder, a doctor, a writer, or something else.

Every morning when you get up ask Jesus to help you make good choices throughout your day. Then you will know Him very well; and when He comes back to take you to heaven, you will be ready to go.

Mirror 1

"As water reflects the face, so one's life reflects the heart."
—Proverbs 27:19, NIV

I have something in my bag that helps us keep clean! Any guesses? (Let the children respond.) What I have in my bag is a mirror. I need to look in a mirror to know if my face is dirty or if my hair is combed (brushed) nicely.

Sometimes we don't like what we see in a mirror, and it makes us unhappy. Can you think of a reason we might not like what we see? Maybe what we see is that we have blemishes on our face. Or maybe we think that we are too skinny or too chubby, or that our hair is too curly or too straight. People can find all sorts of reasons why they think they don't match up to someone else. They end up thinking they are not good enough the way they are. Then there are those who *like* to look in the mirror because they think they are very pretty or very handsome. Some people spend too much time looking at themselves.

When we look in a mirror, we only see what we look like on the outside. But when God looks at us, He pays attention to what is on the inside, to what our hearts and what our minds are like. God doesn't look at how tall, how short, how pretty, or how handsome we are. He looks at how kind, how loving, how helpful, and how honest we are.

The lesson He wants us to learn from how He looks at us is that He values the content of our hearts—not the way we look on the outside. When we make friends, we shouldn't be looking at what others look like on the outside. Instead we should make friends with kids who want to love Jesus as much as we want to and who pray to have the character of Jesus in their hearts.

God loves all of us no matter what we look like. He wants us to continue growing in our love for Him so that when He comes, we will be ready to go to heaven with Him. Remember that God isn't finished with us yet!

Mirror 2

What You Need:
▸ one mirror

"If we confess our sins, he is faithful and just and will forgive us our sins and purify us from all unrighteousness."
—1 John 1:9, NIV

I have something in my bag that looks back at you. Can you guess what it is? *(A mirror.)* Raise your hand if you looked in a mirror today. How did you look this morning? Did you look back at yourself? Have you ever made funny faces at yourself? Does your reflection laugh with you? What if you saw a big spot on your clothes? Would you just forget about it, or would you change into something else?

Is it important for you to like what you see? *(Yes.)* What about how other people see you? Is that important? *(Yes.)* If it is important to like what you see and what other people see in you, is it important what Jesus sees when He looks at you? *(Yes.)*

What if there are dirty spots on the inside where Jesus can see? Are those dirty spots like sin? How can we clean the spots on our insides? (Let the children respond.) We have to admit we did something wrong and that we feel sorry about it, and we have to ask Jesus to clean the spot by forgiving us. Did you know that Jesus not only promises to forgive us of our sins but that He also says that He forgets them? Isn't that a wonderful God?

If you have dirty spots on your clothes, you can change your clothes. If you have dirty spots, or *sin*, in your heart, you can ask for forgiveness, and Jesus will make you clean on the inside.

Next time you look at yourself in the mirror, take a few extra minutes to ask Jesus if there is anything on the inside that needs to be forgiven. Can we go to heaven if we have dirty spots on the inside? *(No.)* God wants us to be in heaven with Him, so remember to be clean on the inside.

What You Need:
- one pair of mittens
- one swimsuit
- one pair of boots
- one photo of a suit of armor

Mittens, Swimsuits, and Boots

"Put on the full armor of God, so that you can take your stand against the devil's schemes."
—Ephesians 6:11, NIV

There are three things in my bag today that each of you might have at home. As I show them to you, take a look at them, and tell me what they should be used for. Let's see if you agree with me when I tell you how I think they should be used.

Here is the first item. What are these? *(Mittens.)* You are right. Mittens are to be put on your hands when you go to the beach in the summer! Do you agree? *(No.)* When *should* you wear mittens? (Let the children respond.)

Next we have a swimsuit. I say a swimsuit should be worn when you go snow skiing. Do you agree? *(No!)* When should you wear a swimsuit? (Let them respond.)

How about this pair of boots? Should we put them on to run a race? *(No.)* You boys and girls are very smart! You know the right clothes to wear at the right times!

I have another question. What do you wear to protect yourself from Satan? Jesus told us to "put on the full armor of God" (Ephesians 6:11, NIV). How many know what a suit of armor looks like? Let me show you a photo. There are metal pants, shoes, a shirt, and a hat.

Do you think that is what Jesus means when He tells us to put on the full armor of God? *(No.)* What do you think the suit of armor is that the Bible talks about? (Let them respond.) I think it means we should read what is written in the Bible, pray, listen to your parents and teachers, study your Sabbath School lesson, and obey the commandments. When you do these things, Jesus will fill you with His love and help you to say "No" when Satan tries to tempt you.

Just like you know what clothes to wear while at the beach, when skiing, or running a race, you must remember to have the protection of God in your heart. Don't let Satan keep you from accepting the promise of heaven.

Nails 1

"It will be made a wasteland, parched and
desolate before me; the whole land will be laid waste
because there is no one who cares."
—Jeremiah 12:11, NIV

What You Need:

► nine nails of different sizes and kinds (look at the rest of story to find the kinds you need to have)
► one twelve-inch nail
► two short pieces of wood (about 1" x 3" x 6")

Today I have several things in my bag to show you. They are all used for the same purpose, but they don't all look the same. Some are short, and some are long. All are made of metal. They are used to hold things together. Can you guess what they are? *(Nails.)* Here are a few of the different sizes and kinds. (Show all but the twelve-inch nail.) Let's look more closely at them.

This one is very short. Do you think it is the right nail to hold these two boards together? *(No.)* It is too short and won't go all the way through the first board. How about this bigger one? *(No.)* Why not? It is too long. This nail is twisted, and this one has a rubber washer at the top. This one is a different color, and this one is a different metal and color.

I have one more in my bag that I have not shown you yet. Maybe it will be just right to nail these two boards together. Do you want to see it? Look how big it is! Can you guess how long it is? Twelve inches—that equals one foot! Have you ever seen a nail this big? Do you think it will work to nail these two boards together? I think it is too big!

Can we compare these nails to you boys and girls? Yes, because they are all different, just like you are all different sizes, colors, and shapes. All these nails are different because they are meant for specific jobs. Jesus has made each of you different, but He has a specific job for you, even though you are still young.

You can be helpers in Sabbath School. If you are good at folding laundry neatly, you can be a big help to your mom. If you are good at cooking, you can help your parents in the kitchen. Maybe you can help your dad by handing him the tools he needs when he is doing a job. If you have younger sisters and brothers, you can help teach them important things. You can be a friend to other boys and girls. Jesus also has a job for you when you get older, just like this big twelve-inch nail.

All you need to do is ask Jesus to guide your life, and He will lead you to the special job that He has for you. Remember that you are special to Jesus, and He knows the talents you have to help you do a good job for Him, just like each nail has a special job.

What You Need:
▶ one nail
▶ one hammer
▶ one piece of wood

Nails 2

"For we are co-workers in God's service;
you are God's field, God's building."
—1 Corinthians 3:9, NIV

I have something in my bag that is very strong. This item is used for many things. Would you like to see it? What is this? *(Nail.)* You are right. What can a nail do? (Let the children respond.) Can it do that by itself? *(No.)* Maybe I'll just push it into this wood with my fingers! (Try.) Maybe it would be better if I hit it with my hand. (Try. Ouch!) That wasn't a good idea, was it? *(No.)* So what do I need to get this nail into this wood? *(Hammer.)* Good idea!

A nail along with a hammer can do lots of things all by itself, right? *(No?)* So what do they need to be useful? They need a hand to hold the nail, and they need a strong arm to hammer the nail into where it should go.

Is there any way we can compare boys and girls with nails? We have seen that in order for the nail and the hammer to be useful, they need someone to work with them.

Big or small, young or old, we can do better if we work together as a team when there is a job to be done. If the nail and the hammer are just lying around, they aren't of much use, just like you are more useful when you are not just lying around. You have your parents and teachers and, best of all, Jesus to help you accomplish great things when you work together as a team. It takes all of us to learn to live like Jesus and to be ready to live with Him in heaven when He comes. I want to see each one of you there.

New Year's Resolutions

What You Need:
➤ one piece of paper with New Year's Resolutions written on it
➤ one pencil or pen

"Each of you should use whatever gift you have received to serve others, as faithful stewards of God's grace in its various forms."
—1 Peter 4:10, NIV

Let's take a look at what I have in my bag today. You can see that it is a piece of paper and a pencil (pen). Let's pretend it is January 1, the first day of a new year. Can you think of any reason why I might use a piece of paper and a pencil (pen) on the first day of the year? Have you ever heard of someone writing down their New Year's resolutions? Sometimes they write short lists; other times the lists are long.

Do you know what a New Year's resolution is? (Let the children respond.) A *resolution* is kind of like a promise—something you decide is important for you to do every day. Is there anyone here who has ever made one? Do you think you should make one?

What are some of the things you would put on your list? (Let them respond.) Sometimes people promise to read their Bibles every morning; sometimes they promise they will spend more time with their families or spend less time watching TV. There are many other promises people make. Would you like to promise Jesus that you will be obedient to Him and to your parents?

If you didn't do everything you promised Jesus you would do, would Jesus forgive you? *(Yes.)* Is it important for you to have a list? *(Maybe.)* Sometimes it helps us to write important things down because we forget easily. If we write our ideas down, we can review them from time to time and be reminded of the things we wrote. But if you don't make a list, how can you remember the things that are important for you to do every day? Could you ask Jesus to remind you? *(Yes.)*

It might be a good idea to sit down with your parents to talk about some of the important things you should include in your everyday activities—not just the things you want to do for Jesus, but also for your mom and dad, your sisters and brothers, and your friends.

North, South, East, West

"As far as the east is from the west,
so far has he removed our sins from us."
—Psalm 103:12, NABRE

Raise your hand if you learned something in Sabbath School this morning. Did all of you learn something new this week? I know you are all very smart. That is why I need help this morning. So put on your thinking caps, and see if you can answer my question.

Everybody stand up, but not too close to the friend next to you. Think, now, before you show me your answer. Don't pay any attention to how your friends answer. Here is the question. Can you point to the direction of *south*? (Look around.) Is everyone pointing in the same direction? *(No.)* Let's try another direction. Can you point to *north*? I checked before church started, and *north* is this direction. (Point north.) Did everyone guess correctly? *(No.)* Now that we know which way is north, can you figure out which way is east? Now the west? The way I remember the direction of east and west is that west is always on my left if I am facing north. The opposite from *west* is *east*, so east would be on my right side. What did I say about how you can tell where west is? *(It is to my left.)*

Now that you know how to find east and west, how do you find the direction of north? I have something in my bag that always points north, no matter what direction you are facing. Do you know what it is? *(Compass.)* The compass is a great help! If you go on a hike, you should always take a compass to guide you, so you won't get lost.

There is an interesting verse in the Bible about east and west that I'd like to tell you about: Psalm 103:12. When you ask forgiveness for your sins, David says, "As far as the east is from the west, so far has he removed our sins from us" (Psalm 103:12, NABRE). East never meets west, so that means we don't have to worry about those past sins. God has taken them away and remembers them no more!

Just as you can depend on your compass always pointing north, you can also depend on God's promise that when you are sorry for your sins and you ask Him to forgive you, He does just that, and it is gone forever.

Raise your hand if you want God to remove your sins as far away as the east is from the west. Do you remember which way is west? (Have the children point.) Good. God loves each of you boys and girls!

Offering for God

What You Need:
▶ money—bills and coins

"But seek first his kingdom and his righteousness,
and all these things will be given to you as well."
—Matthew 6:33, NIV

Today my bag has something that is made from paper and that is made from metal. And it is something that all of you have held in your hands. Raise your hand if you think you know what it is. Sometimes it is green; and in some places, the color and the size are different. *(Money.)*

Did any of you boys and girls bring money to church today? Maybe your parents gave you some money to bring to Sabbath School as an offering for Jesus.

When you think about the things you are given, do you remember to thank Jesus for them? Who can tell me about something special that Jesus provides for you?

Do you think you can buy God's love? *(No.)* It is a free gift! Did you know that He blesses us with more gifts than we know what to do with? Sometimes we forget to thank Him. I am sure He appreciates it when we do remember to say, "Thank You!" When is a good time to thank Him? First thing when we get up in the morning! Is that the only time? *(No.)*

A good prayer in the morning is, "Dear Jesus, help me today to do what You want me to do." If you really mean what you pray, God will bless you. Do you believe that? I hope and pray you do.

Let me tell you something about offerings. Some people make a promise with God that if God will do what they have prayed for, they will make Him a special gift. I knew a man who planted a big garden, and he told God he would give all the money he received from selling tomatoes from the one special row. He had lots of other rows of tomatoes, but this one was special. He worked hard on all of the rows, but God was going to have to do the rest. Do you think God did? *(Yes.)* All the other rows produced lots of tomatoes, but this one special row grew bigger and more tomatoes than the other rows. God blessed his investment tomatoes. He had lots of money to give to God.

I hope you will remember to ask God to bless you, and then you will be able to give gifts to God.

Olympic Gold Medal (Remember the Gold)

"Blessed is the one who perseveres under trial because, having stood the test, that person will receive the crown of life that the Lord has promised to those who love him."
—James 1:12, NIV

I have something in my bag that a lot of young men and women would love to have. Those who receive one usually start trying for it when they are young, and they have to work very hard to prepare. If they get one, it is another four years before they can try for another. Can you guess what it is? *(Olympic medal.)*

There are three kinds of Olympic medals. Do you know what they are? A bronze, silver, and gold. Which is the one that everyone wants to receive? The gold one! Have you ever watched the Olympics on TV? I am always proud of the young men and women who represent the United States of America. I would like to tell you just a little about how hard those young men and women work to win the gold.

One young man swims eighty kilometers, about fifty miles every week. He spends seven hours a day in the pool. One girl spent fourteen years training in the pool. She started at the age of two. Another young man left home at the age of six to attend a training school for gymnastics in Russia. He was only allowed to go home for two days, two times a month. He is now seventeen, and he won a gold medal. All of these young boys and girls have grown up with one goal: to be the best they can be in their sport and to win the gold medal.

There is something that all of us, children and grown-ups, are working for every day, and it is not a gold medal. Do you know what it is? Jesus is waiting to give us gold crowns when we go to heaven. Is going to church once a week enough to earn the gold crown? *(No.)* If young people work for hours every day for many years just to win a gold medal, should we do less for Jesus and heaven? *(No.)*

However, working for Jesus is *not* how you will get to heaven! How do you get there? What you do is give Jesus your heart and live the way He guides you every day. Ask Him to forgive your sins and to help you to stop sinning. The "work" is remembering to stay with Jesus all day long. When you do that, heaven is a *gift* from Jesus.

Olympic winners have coaches that work with them every day to help them win their medals. I pray that you will talk with Jesus as soon as you wake up and that you will let Him coach you every hour of every day. Let Him teach you how to live a life like His.

How many want to win heaven's gold? I want to be there with you.

Paper Bridge

"Follow God's example, therefore, as dearly loved children and walk in the way of love, just as Christ loved us and gave himself up for us as a fragrant offering and sacrifice to God."
—Ephesians 5:1, 2, NIV

What You Need:
- two 8½" x 11" sheets of paper, flat sheet folded ½" lengthwise like a fan
- two books
- one empty glass (test beforehand)

Raise your hand if you have ever tried to do something you weren't able to do. Can you think of something you tried and couldn't do? Were you able to do it when you got someone to help you?

Let me show you an example of how, sometimes with a little help, you can do more. Let's pretend these two books are mountains and that we want to build a bridge across them. Now let's pretend this piece of paper is a bridge. That looks pretty good to me. Do you think the bridge will hold this glass on it? *(No.)* Let's see if I can help this piece of paper to be a better bridge. (Use folded sheet of paper.) Now let's try again. Do you think it will work this time?

You boys and girls are kind of like the piece of paper. Do you want to know how? If you let Jesus and your parents help you mold your life, shaping it like I did the paper, you will become a better person when you grow up. Jesus will also help your parents to be stronger just like my paper bridge. All we have to do is ask Jesus to come into our lives and mold us to be more like Him.

I hope each of you will start each morning by praying and asking Jesus to mold you to be like Him.

What You Need:
- paper clips
- the word *Jesus* on a sheet of paper
- the word *Friend* on a sheet of paper

Paper Clips

"His master replied, 'Well done, good and faithful servant! You have been faithful with a few things; I will put you in charge of many things. Come and share your master's happiness!' "

—Matthew 25:21, NIV

I have something in my bag that is metal. It isn't very big. It used to be straight, but it has been bent into a special shape. Sometimes it is quite small, other times it is bigger but not too large. If you were to change the shape back to straight, it wouldn't be of much use for what it is intended. Does anyone want to make a guess? *(Paper clip.)*

Have you ever used paper clips? What are they used for? (Let the children respond.) Mostly, they are used to clip papers together. If I bend one apart, will it still work? *(No.)* This is the only way it will work to keep things together.

Christian boys and girls are a little like paper clips. Does that sound funny? How could you be like paper clips? Paper clips are useful when they are shaped into the form that will hold papers together. When boys and girls live the way Jesus wants them to live, they are very useful. But if they decide to do what Satan tempts them to do, it is like bending this paper clip to the side.

Jesus wants us to hold our friends close together with Him. Let me show you! (Clip two sheets of paper together, one with the word *Jesus* and the other with the word *Friend*.) If we bring a friend together with Jesus, He will use you to help that friend know Him better. If we let Satan pull us apart, can we keep Jesus close to us? *(No.)* See what happens when I bend the paper clip. Your friend will slip away from Jesus.

I'm praying you will ask Jesus every day to help you stay in the right shape to keep Him close to you! The best way to do that is to pray to Him every day.

Patience

"But if we hope for what we do not yet have,
we wait for it patiently."
—Romans 8:25, NIV

What You Need:
➤ one metronome
➤ one egg timer
➤ one stopwatch
➤ one alarm clock, watch, or any other time keeper

Have you ever wanted something very much? Did you get what you wanted right away? Have your parents ever said, "Be patient and wait"? Have you ever been told to wait thirty minutes or an hour? How do you keep track of time? Maybe you had to ask if it was time yet. Have you ever asked, "How much longer?" I brought a few things that can help you keep track of time. Each one is different, but all are important.

Metronome. You can set it to the speed that you want. Is there anyone here who is taking piano lessons? Do you know what a metronome is used for? *(Keeping time with music.)*

Egg timer. How does this egg timer work? Do you know what it is used for? *(You turn it over, and when the sand completely runs down, the eggs are cooked.)*

Stopwatch. Do you know what it is used for? If you are running a race, you can see how long it takes you to get from the starting line to the finish line.

Alarm clock. Do you know what it is used for? You can set it to ring at a certain time, such as when you want to get up in the morning.

God wants us to learn to be patient. He knows the best time for something to take place. Learning to wait for what your parents have promised or for what God has promised to happen will teach you patience.

(Read Romans 8:25.) Sometimes you want something—right now! When your parents say, "No," you must learn to patiently wait. That will help you to patiently wait for God to answer your prayers. He knows the best time to answer.

Peanuts

" 'For I know the plans I have for you,' declares the LORD,
'plans to prosper you and not to harm you,
plans to give you hope and a future.' "
—Jeremiah 29:11, NIV

I have something in my bag that reminds me of you boys and girls. Do you want a clue? They are all the same but all are a little different. The outside has a protective covering, like a banana, but what is inside is something some kids like to eat. Can anyone guess? (Let the children respond.) *(Peanuts.)*

Do you know why they remind me of you boys and girls? You are all different sizes and shapes, but on the inside, you each have something that is the same. Can you guess? You have invited Jesus to live in your heart and mind! God looks on the inside of each of us, just like we look on the inside of the peanut for the good part of it.

Do you know how many things you can make with a peanut? The last time I checked, it was 375! A man named George Washington Carver decided the peanut was very important, so he experimented to see how many things he could make from peanuts.

God works with each of you in somewhat the same way. There are many things He can use you to do as you are growing up. God has a plan for you, and you need to pray and ask Him every day to show you what that plan is. You can also find many clues from God's Word, the Bible. Your parents can also help you decide what you can do for Jesus.

I want to give each of you two peanuts. One you can eat after church *if* you are not allergic to peanuts, and the other is to keep beside your bed to remind you that God has a special plan for you.

Pearls

What You Need:
▸ one photo of an oyster
▸ pearls (or a photo of pearls)

"Bless those who persecute you; bless and do not curse."
—Romans 12:14, NIV
"When he found one of great value, he went away and sold
everything he had and bought it."
—Matthew 13:46, NIV

What I have in my bag today is something that is considered to be precious and very valuable. Do you know what that word *valuable* means? *Valuable* means that these things can cost a lot on money. Need a clue? It is something that is in the ocean, and inside of it is something that grows. Does anyone have any idea what it might be? *(Pearl.)* (Show the pearl or a photo.) Isn't it beautiful?

Do you know where this pearl came from? *(An oyster.)* (Show photo.) Here is a photo of an oyster. It isn't very pretty, is it? An oyster is called a "mollusk." How does a beautiful pearl come from such an ugly mollusk? Do you know what makes the oyster create a pearl? A grain of sand somehow gets inside the shell of the oyster, and because the sand doesn't belong there, the oyster wants to get rid of it. The oyster can't get rid of it, so it covers it up and rolls it around in the shell. The sand gets bigger and bigger as it is rolled around and eventually becomes a pearl. There are people who "grow" oysters who know how long to let them grow before they collect them from the ocean. Then they open them up to see if there are nice pearls on the inside.

Isn't it amazing how one small grain of sand can grow into a beautiful pearl? That is one of the special miracles God has for us to see.

The little grain of sand that gets into the shell of the oyster is irritating to the oyster, and that is why it covers it up. Sometimes God allows trials to get into our lives like the sand gets into the oyster. Have you ever had a small rock get into your shoe? It is irritating and hurts, doesn't it? Sometimes kids who are supposed to be our friends say things to us that hurt our feelings. Jesus tells us to love those that hurt us and to be an example to them, just like He is our example. He wants us to grow into loving Christians, so we will be ready to go to heaven with Him when He comes.

Did you know that the Bible tells us there will be pearls in heaven? In Revelation 21:21, it says that there will be twelve gates, and each gate is made from one pearl. Can you imagine how big one pearl has to get to be big enough to make a gate? I know I want to see that. Raise your hand if you want to see the gates of pearl, not only to see them, but also to walk through those pearly gates into heaven.

What You Need:

▸ pencils—some unsharpened, some sharpened

Pencils

"Even small children are known by their actions,
so is their conduct really pure and upright?"
—Proverbs 20:11, NIV

Raise your hand if you would like to know what I have in my bag today. Before I show you, I'll give you some clues. It is soft on one end and hard on the other end. Do you need another clue? OK, it can be either short or long. It can be round, or it can be another shape. Sometimes it is yellow, but it also comes in many other colors. Now can you guess? *(Pencil.)*

Pencils are made with a lot of differences, but they all have something in common that makes them alike. In what way are all pencils the same? *(They all have lead in them. They all have to be sharpened in order to write with them.)*

Let's talk about how pencils are like boys and girls. It's true. Boys and girls are all sizes, shapes, and colors; but what do they all have in common? (Let the children respond.) It is this! Never forget that you are all the same because Jesus loves you. You are all His special boys and girls. Let's see. I'm going to choose one of these pencils. Does it matter which pencil I use? (If they say, "No," pick up an unsharpened one. If they say, "Yes," pick up a sharpened one.)

Do you know how Jesus "sharpens" you and me so He can use us? He gives us His Word, the Bible, which helps us learn how He wants us to live.

As you can see, I have a sharpened pencil in my hand. (Lay it flat in your hand.) What can this pencil do now that it is lying on my hand? *(Nothing.)* What needs to happen for this pencil to be useful? (If someone says, "Lift it up," just raise the hand with the pencil in it up higher.) OK. Can it be used now? *(No!)* What way must it be held to be useful? (If someone says, "Straight up," hold it in a fist.) Does it matter which end is up? *(Yes.)* The point must be down. Now can I use it? What happens now when I touch the paper with it? It makes a mark!

Did you know that you boys and girls are like pencils in another way? Everything you say or do leaves a mark, an impression, on someone. You can make people happy or sad. Did you also know that something on this pencil is like Jesus? The eraser removes the bad marks, like when Jesus forgives and erases your sins.

How important is it to hold the pencil just right? If we don't hold it correctly, it doesn't work. Just like this pencil must be held tightly in your hand, you need to pray every day for Jesus to hold you tight and lead you in everything you do and say.

Pennies

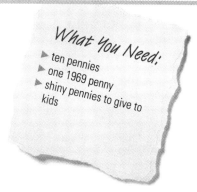

"In the same way, let your light shine before others, that they may see your good deeds and glorify your Father in heaven."
—Matthew 5:16, NIV

I have ten things in my bag. All of them are the same, but half of them look different. They are all made from copper and are all worth the same. Want to take a guess? *(Pennies.)*

Let's see how half are different. The dates the pennies were made are not all in the same year. Were you boys and girls all born in the same year? *(No.)* Well, that's something you have in common with the pennies.

Let's discover why half are the same but look different. Here is a shiny penny, and here is a dull penny. If you keep Jesus in your hearts, you will be like this shiny penny, letting your light shine. But if Satan enters your heart, you become dull with sin.

When you get older like this 1969 penny, you may not look as shiny on the outside as these new pennies look, but you can still be shiny on the inside.

How are these coins all the same? They are all pennies. All of you boys and girls are worth the same in Jesus' eyes. He died for each one of you.

My prayer is that each of you will remain shiny as you keep Jesus close by your side. Pray for Him to be in your heart every day so that you will be ready to go to heaven with Him when He comes.

I am going to give each of you a shiny penny to put on your dresser to remind you to pray every day to ask Jesus for help in keeping you shiny!

Piggy Bank

"Finally, brothers and sisters, whatever is true, whatever is noble, whatever is right, whatever is pure, whatever is lovely, whatever is admirable—if anything is excellent or praiseworthy—think about such things."

—Philippians 4:8, NIV

I have something in my bag that has an opening on the top so that something can be put inside. Sometimes it gets shaken when you want to discover if it is getting full yet. Can you guess what it is? Do you need another clue? They come in all sizes, shapes, and colors. Sometimes people open one and take out what is inside of it. *(Piggy bank.)*

Raise your hand if you have piggy bank or some kind of bank to keep your money in at home. Can you see the money, or is it hidden? Do you shake it to see how full it is? Have you ever opened it and taken the money out? Would you rather save your money or spend it? Would you ever put pieces of plain paper in it to fill it up? What about putting soda can tabs in it? *(No.)* Why? *(Because you can't buy anything with plain paper or can tabs.)*

Let's compare your brain with a bank. Your brain remembers the things you see and hear. It's called your "memory." It keeps track of all the good things you learn. Unfortunately, it also remembers the not-so-good things.

What if you put one dollar in your bank this week and then just a plain piece of paper the next week? And if you kept doing that, when the bank filled up, it would only be half full of money. The other half—full of just plain paper—wouldn't be of any value, right?

Jesus doesn't want you to fill your brain with junk, things that are not worth anything. He wants your brain to remember all the good things you know from learning about Him.

I pray each of you will be careful of what you look at, what you listen to, and what things you play with so that you can fill your brain with valuable things that will help you as you grow to be like Jesus.

Pillow, Robe, and Blanket

"Indeed, he who watches over Israel will neither
slumber nor sleep. The Lord watches over you—
the Lord is your shade at your right hand;
the sun will not harm you by day, nor the moon by night."
—Psalm 121:4–6, NIV

Raise your hand if you played a lot this week. Playing hard uses a lot of energy and makes you want to rest. Are you tired today? I am *so* glad Jesus gave us the Sabbath, a rest day. On Sabbath, we can do more than rest; we can remember all that He created for us and to take time to thank Him for loving us so much.

I am tired today, so I put some things in my bag that you probably also have at your house, at least something similar. When you get tired at home, what do you do? (Let the children respond.) *(Go to sleep.)* The things in my bag are things you use when you are going to lie down. Can you guess what they are? (Let them respond.) When you rest, where is your head? *(On a pillow.)* There are two other things that I use to help me rest: my robe and my blanket.

Now I am all ready to stop my story and take a nap. Is that OK with you? Can you boys and girls sit there and take care of yourselves while I take a nap?

Who do you think takes care of us while God takes a nap? Do you think God does or doesn't take naps? Let's see what the Bible says about that. (Read Psalm 121:4–6.)

Does that mean He will protect you if something scares you in the middle of the night? *(Yes.)* Can you pray for help when you are crying? *(Yes.)* Can you trust God to always be there when you need Him? *(Yes.)* Remember that God is always watching over you, day and night.

Pinecone Core

"I have hidden your word in my heart that I might not sin against you."
—Psalm 119:11, NIV

If you live in an area where there are pine trees, what I have in my bag is something you see a lot of throughout the year. Would you like to see what I have? Can you tell me what it is? A pinecone core. (If they do not recognize it, show them the pieces and branches also.)

Do you know what makes this pinecone core special? All the branches have been picked off. That means it has been pulled apart. Do you know how that happened? Squirrels do this so that they can eat the seed, the pine nut. They take the yummy part out of the pinecone.

Have you seen squirrels take pinecones apart? They break each branch off and put the seeds in their mouths. They will put so many seeds in their mouths that their cheeks will bulge out on both sides. Do you know what they do next with the nuts? They bury them in the ground, so they can go back and eat them in the winter. If the squirrels didn't work hard to get the nuts out of the pinecones, they would not have enough food to eat during the winter.

Did you know that God has given each of us something special to work hard at getting the "yummy" information from? Do you know what it is? The Bible! Of course, we don't literally eat the Bible. But the Bible is full of important stories and things that we need to learn.

If you just leave your Bible on the shelf, will you be able to get the good out of it? *(No.)* If we just carry it to church, will we get the good out of it? *(No.)* Like the squirrel prepares for winter by burying the tasty nuts, we need to read, study, and learn all the good news the Bible has for us to prepare us for heaven. We want our Bibles to look like this pinecone—well used! If you study your Bible so much that you wear out the pages, you can get another one, just like the squirrel searches for a new pinecone. I hope each of you will learn what Jesus has to tell you as you study your Bible.

Pine and Apple Seeds

"He replied, 'If you have faith as small as a mustard seed,
you can say to this mulberry tree,
"Be uprooted and planted in the sea,"
and it will obey you.' "
—Luke 17:6, NIV

I have some things in my bag that come in different sizes; sometimes they are small and sometimes very big. Most of the time they are brown, but they can also be green. Some people use them for Christmas decorations. Can you guess what I have? *(Pinecones.)* (Show the children.) You can see they are different sizes, just like you boys and girls.

Did you know there is something on the inside of each pinecone that is special? Can you guess what it is? *(Seeds.)* They are called "pine nuts," and they are good to eat. There is one animal that really likes them. What animal do you think it is? *(Squirrel.)* A squirrel will tear a pinecone apart to get the seeds out and eat them.

When a pine seed is planted, what do you think will grow? *(A pine tree.)* What if I plant an apple seed? Will it grow a pine tree? *(No.)* What will grow? *(An apple tree.)*

Did you know there is a special seed inside each one of you boys and girls? It is called "faith." Do you know what that means? It means that Jesus has planted in your heart a seed of faith so that we can believe things that we cannot see. When you plant an apple seed, you have faith that an apple tree will grow. When you plant a pine seed, you have faith that a pine tree will grow. When Jesus planted a seed of faith in your heart, it helps you to believe in Him, even though we cannot see Him face to face. If we "plant" Jesus in our hearts by reading our Bibles and praying, we will grow closer and closer to Him. He wants to fill your heart with joy and happiness.

How many of you boys and girls want the seed of faith in Jesus to grow in you?

What You Need:
- unpopped popcorn in a jar
- one package of microwave popcorn
- salt
- butter

Popcorn

"Taste and see that the LORD is good;
blessed is the one who takes refuge in him."
—Psalm 34:8, NIV

I have something in my bag that most boys and girls like to eat. Would you like to see what I have? (Show the children the jar.) What is it? Popcorn! Would you like to eat this now? *(No.)* Why not? *(Because it's not popped!)* What do I have to do to pop it? *(Heat it up!)* Should I put the *whole* jar on the stove or in the microwave? *(No.)* Can I just pour some out into the microwave? *(No.)*

(Show them the microwave popcorn bag.) What if I use one of these packages in the microwave? After it has popped, is it ready to eat? Sometimes Yes, and sometimes No. The reason is that some microwave popcorn is just plain, with nothing on it. What do you think it might need to taste better? *(Salt and butter.)* That makes the popcorn taste better. Some microwave popcorn already has the butter and salt in the bag.

Let's compare you boys and girls with popcorn! When you are born, are you ready to get a job and work? *(No.)* What do you have to do? You have to grow first. You have to learn to eat, learn to walk, learn to talk—so much growing you have to do before you are ready to get a job. That is like heating the popcorn. There are steps you have to take before popcorn becomes ready to eat. It takes time. As you get older, you will learn to study and go to school.

Growing up is like the popcorn when it pops. After the popcorn is popped, it needs a little salt and butter to make it taste better. Learning about Jesus and His love for you is like having the salt and butter on the popcorn. Having Jesus in your heart helps you to become kinder, sweeter, more loving, and more helpful to others. Let's pray that you will grow to be more like Jesus, so you can be in heaven with Him to taste and see that He is good!

Big and Little Job Power

What You Need:
➤ one steel rod
➤ one wooden stake
➤ one small hammer
➤ one sledgehammer
➤ one toothpick

"After they prayed, the place where they were meeting was
shaken. And they were all filled with the Holy Spirit
and spoke the word of God boldly."
—Acts 4:31, NIV

Raise your hand if you think you are pretty strong. Do you have muscles in your hands and arms? I have something in my bag that needs to be pounded into the ground. (Show the children the rod and the stake.) This is a rod made from steel, and this is a stake made from wood. Does anyone here think they are strong enough and have the power to pound either of these into the ground with their hands? *(No.)* What do you need to pound these things into the ground? *(A hammer.)* (Bring out the very small hammer.) Will this work? *(No.)* Why? (Let the children respond.) What do you need? *(A bigger hammer.)* OK, I have one that I think will do the job! (Show them the sledgehammer.) Will this work? *(Yes.)*

I have something else that I want to pound into the ground. (Show them the toothpick.) Do you think this big sledgehammer will do the job? *(No.)* Why? (Let them respond.) Yes, this hammer is too big.

When you need a lot of power either for big or little jobs, you need to call on Jesus for help. He has all the power you need. All you have to do is ask for it. When you are tempted to tell a lie or to say something bad about your brother or sister, you can stop and *ask* Jesus to supply the power you need to not make those mistakes. Jesus sends a Helper to you, the Holy Spirit, who is with you to help you whenever you ask (Acts 4:31).

How do we get the power we need? *(We pray to Jesus.)* How many want to be filled with the power that Jesus supplies through the Holy Spirit? Remember to pray and ask!

What You Need:

► one jar labeled Prayer Jar
► one jar labeled Answered Prayer Jar
► write some answered prayers and unanswered prayers on slips of paper, and place them in the jars

Prayer Jars

"And I will do whatever you ask in my name,
so that the Father may be glorified in the Son.
You may ask me for anything in my name, and I will do it."
—John 14:13, 14, NIV

Let me show you what I have in my bag today. They are made of glass, and they are the same except that they are labeled differently. (Show the children the jars.) These are not just any jars; these two jars have a special purpose. Can you see the label on each jar? Raise your hand if you can read the words on the labels. (Choose someone to read the labels.) One is my prayer jar, the jar I put prayer requests into. The other is my answered-prayer jar. Raise your hand if you have prayer jars at home or some other method to keep track of the prayer requests you ask of Jesus.

This is how it works. Every morning at worship, write down your special prayer for that day. If you have more than one special prayer, then write it on a separate piece of paper. If you can't write, ask one of your parents to do it for you. Then *stop* and *pray*, asking Jesus to answer your prayer. After praying, fold the paper and drop it in the unanswered prayer jar. If you want, you can write your prayer on two pieces of paper and put one in your pocket to remind you throughout the day to pray again.

In the evening before you go to bed, take a look at the papers in your unanswered prayer jar to see if your request has been answered. If it has, then place it in your answered prayer jar, and thank Jesus for His answer. If it is still unanswered, pray again, and put it back in the prayer jar.

It is very *important* that when you ask Jesus for an answer to your request that you also ask that He answer according to *His will*. The reason for that is Jesus always knows what is best for us. Sometimes we ask for things we do not need or for something selfish. His answer may be "No" if He knows it is not the best for us.

It will be so much fun to see how Jesus answers your prayers. No one loves you more than He does. He always knows the best time to answer your prayer, so be patient. It may take a while. Ask your mom or dad to help you make your prayer jars. Don't forget to thank Jesus when your prayer has been answered.

Rewards

What You Need:
▶ make one sign offering a $100 reward for a lost gold watch
▶ one treat to reward each child

"Look, I am coming soon! My reward is with me, and I will give
to each person according to what they have done."
—Revelation 22:12, NIV

I have something in my bag that is offering something valuable. Would you like to see it? Raise your hand if you can read what is on my sign. (Choose someone to read, "$100 reward for the return of my gold watch.") Would any of you be interested in looking for my watch? Would it be nice to receive one hundred dollars for finding it?

Have you ever been offered a reward? Have your parents ever offered you something if you did what they asked you to do? Have you ever had an offer of a trip to an ice-cream shop as a reward for cleaning your room? Is that a reward?

Did you know there is a special reward mentioned in the Bible? Revelation 22:12 tells us that Jesus has promised that He is coming soon and that He will bring a reward with Him. Do you know what that reward is? (Let the children respond.) Heaven and life eternal! We will be able to live with Jesus, God the Father, and the Holy Spirit in a wonderful place forever. Does that sound like a reward you are interested in?

I have a reward for you today! These are treats for each of you to eat, but you have to promise not to eat them until your parents say it is OK. Do you know why I am giving them to you? Is it just because you came up to listen to my story? I'm glad you came to listen, but I have another reason why I'm giving them to you. The reason is that there is a problem with my reward. It won't last forever! When you put it in your mouth, it will be good for a short time, and then it will be gone.

Is my reward as good as Jesus' reward? (No.) Is His reward better than what I have given you? (Yes!) Raise your hand if you want what Jesus is offering. What must we do to receive Jesus' reward? Keep His commandments and study and pray every day.

I hope you will remember that all rewards on this earth only last a short time, but Jesus' reward will last forever!

What You Need:
▸ rubber bands, save one out

Rubber Bands

"And lead us not into temptation,
but deliver us from the evil one."
—Matthew 6:13, NIV

Raise your hand if you think you are strong. I have something in my bag that can test how strong you are. Who can tell me what this is? *(A rubber band.)* How many of you think you can stretch this rubber band? OK, it looks like all of you think you are strong enough to stretch it. I agree. I think you can too! I have more rubber bands in my bag. Do you want to see them? They are all the same size as the first one. Raise your hand if you think you can stretch this group of rubber bands. Do I have a volunteer? Give it a try. Is it too hard? Let's see if the two of us can stretch it. It's still hard; but with two of us, it is easier.

Did you know you can compare sin with this group of rubber bands? Sometimes when Satan tempts you to sin, it is easy to say "No" to him if it is just a small temptation. But sometimes Satan tempts us with things that are not so easy to say "No" to. He knows the things that tempt you the most; and even when you know it is wrong, it is hard for you to say "No."

Those are times when you need help from Jesus, just as it took two of us to stretch the group of rubber bands. How can we get help from Jesus? All we have to do is *ask*, and He will send His angels. Sometimes the angels are your parents, sometimes they are your teachers, and sometimes they are your friends. Jesus knows what help you need. When you ask, He steps right in between you and Satan and will give you the help you need to resist the temptation.

I hope the next time that Satan tempts you to sin, you will stop and pray to Jesus for help to fight Satan off!

Salt

What You Need:
- salt

"Salt is good, but if it loses its saltiness,
how can you make it salty again?
Have salt among yourselves,
and be at peace with each other."
—Mark 9:50, NIV

I have something in my bag that you can either see or not see. Confused? Sometimes it has a good taste, and sometimes it has a bad taste. This is a hard one! Let me give you a few clues. When you are eating french fries, they taste better with this on them. Does anyone want to take a guess? *(Salt.)* When can you see salt? *(When it is dry.)* What happens when salt gets wet? Can you still see it? *(No.)* Why? *(Because it dissolves.)* Have you ever been to the ocean and got saltwater in your mouth? Did it taste good? *(No.)* What did it taste like? *(Salt.)* Really strong salt! Salt is really good when it flavors the food you eat. But have you ever eaten cooked oatmeal that hasn't been salted? It doesn't taste as good as it does when there is a little salt to flavor it. If there is not enough salt, food doesn't taste very good; and if there is too much salt, the food tastes too strong.

Let's compare salt with Christians. When you boys and girls fall in love with Jesus, it is natural for you to want to become like Him. And if we are like Jesus, we will want to help others learn to love Him also. No one can get to heaven by doing good things. Heaven is a gift that Jesus offers us for free. The good things are important for us to do because when we love Jesus, we will want to do good things, just as He did. When people see that you are helping Jesus by helping others, it is like the salt that is dry—we can see it. We can say, "Wow, she must really love Jesus because she is always doing something nice for someone."

Jesus wants each of you to read about what He did while He was here on this earth. He loved everyone He met, even the ones who didn't treat Him right. The Bible shows us how to follow Jesus and accept the gift of heaven.

If you ask Jesus to be with you all the time—at home, at school, at church, or when you are playing with your family or friends—He will answer your prayer and will be with you. He says if you want Him to be in your life, He will never leave you.

Raise your hand if you want to ask Jesus into your heart. When Jesus is in our hearts, we will be like the salt that we cannot see. When it melts in our hearts, we will be flavored inside and out. We need to be like dry *and* wet salt to be happy Christians.

Scars

"A gentle answer turns away wrath,
but a harsh word stirs up anger."
—Proverbs 15:1, NIV

Raise your hand if you have ever had someone say something to you that hurt your feelings. Have you ever done or said something that was unkind or that made a friend cry?

I want to tell you a story about a little girl named Hazel, who had a very bad temper. Do you know what a bad temper is? A person with a bad temper always seems to be in an bad mood and does things that hurt others. Hazel's temper was so bad that she often made at least one of her playmates cry. It wasn't long before no one wanted to be with Hazel because of her temper.

Hazel's father decided he had to help her get control of her temper. He got a hammer and a nail and led her outside. He said to her, "Hazel, I want you to control yourself when you get angry. Every time you lose your temper, I will hammer a nail in the gate. (Hammer a nail in the board.) This will remind you of how you are acting. On the days that you control your temper all day and act nicely, I will *remove* a nail."

What do you think happened? At first, Hazel just didn't pay much attention to all the nails in the gate, and pretty soon there were several. (Hammer several more nails in the board.) Hazel began to realize that if she ever wanted to have a friend, she would have to change. One day she decided to be nice all day. When she got home, she told her father that she had been nice, and he took out one nail. (Take one nail out.) Do you think she was always nice after that? *(No.)* She had such a habit of not being nice that nails in the gate were added often. (Hammer a few more nails in the board.) Finally, she realized she needed Jesus in her life, so she started *praying* every morning when she got up. She asked Jesus to help her to always remember to be kind and not angry. It took some time, but eventually her dad was able to remove all of the nails from the gate. (Take all the nails out.)

We need to remember that even when Jesus helps with our problems, we need to ask Him to forgive us and also to ask for forgiveness from the friends we have hurt. Your bad words will leave scars in the minds of your friends if you don't ask them to forgive you. Look at the board we put the nails in. See the scars in the wood? Just as when Jesus died on the cross for our sins, the scars are still in His hands, feet, and side to remind us just how much He loves us and is willing to forgive our sins.

Signature of a Christian

"I am the good shepherd; I know my sheep
and my sheep know me."
—John 10:14, NIV

What You Need:
▶ several sheets of paper folded in half—one folded with your signature in red, and some of the remaining sheets with other's names in red
▶ extra sheets for each child to take

I have several things in my bag that are all the same but are all different. Let me show them to you. (Unfold the piece of paper with your name on it.) Can you tell me how they are all the same? (*All are white paper. [Some may note the red writing.]*) Can you tell me another way they are all the same? (*They all have writing on the inside.*) Yes, they all have writing on the inside; but that isn't what I am thinking of. (Show the children that the names are all different.) Having names written on the inside makes them different in a way, but you could say they are the same because all *have* names on the inside. What makes *mine* different? It is *my* signature. All the others have names, but only *I* can write my signature. If *I* write *your* name on one, is it *your* signature? (*No.*) You are the *only* one who can write your signature.

Do you think God has a signature? (*Yes.*) We cannot actually see God's handwriting in a signature, but we see God's "signature" in the things He has created for us to enjoy. What things can you think of? (Let the children respond.) (*Flowers, birds, trees, mountains, ocean, animals, babies, you, and me.*) All of these were made by God to show us His signature of love. They are all different, but they are all the same because they show us His signature.

I'm giving each of you a piece of paper to write your signature on this afternoon. Ask your mom or dad if you need help. After you write your signature, make a list of things that represent God's signature on the other side of the paper.

Did you know that others recognize your "signature" in the way you act? If you love and follow Jesus, you will have a signature of kindness and love for others. Remember, your words and actions are part of your signature.

Sharp Rocks and Smooth Stones

"Whose paths are crooked and who are devious in their ways."
—Proverbs 2:15, NIV

I have several things in my bag. Some are small, and some are larger. They are all hard. Some have sharp points, and some are smooth. Some are shiny, and some are dull. One place you can find them is in streams of water. Can you guess what they are? *(Rocks and stones.)*

Would you like to know what I think about when I look at rocks and stones? I think about boys and girls your age and about boys and girls my age. Well, we are not boys and girls anymore, are we? Why do you think rocks make me think about people? People are all different sizes and colors.

Some people's personalities are easygoing, smooth, and shiny; others are sharp and jagged. If you had to carry either a sharp rock or a smooth rock in your hand or pocket all day, which would be better—the sharp or the smooth one? Why? (Let the children respond.) The sharp rock will poke your skin or make holes in your pockets. If you had to choose between a smooth, shiny rock and a sharp, jagged rock to put on your dresser, which would you choose? *(Shiny.)*

Do you think God made these smooth and shiny rocks the way they are now? *(No.)* All of these rocks used to be larger and have sharp points. Do you know how they became smooth and shiny? Often, smooth rocks come from a river or from the ocean where the water has rolled them over and over, causing them to rub against other rocks until all the sharp points have worn off. These little stones were put in a small machine full of sand, and the stones were tumbled over and over against the sand until all the sharp edges became smooth; and they became polished rocks.

Did you know that Jesus has a way to remove the sharp edges of our personalities to help us become "smooth and shiny." How can He do that? Several ways! Jesus gave His children the Ten Commandments, which are a guide for us to become good people. The Bible has stories that teach us right from wrong. Your parents can also help to teach you the right way to live. All of these things are helpers to smooth out our sharp edges.

If we pray every day—asking Jesus to take away our rough edges—we will become like shiny rocks and will be ready for Him to take us to heaven. Raise your hand if you want to be with Jesus in heaven. Pray for His help.

Small Print and a Magnifying Glass

"Remember to extol his work,
which people have praised in song."
—Job 36:24, NIV

What You Need:
▸ two small pieces of paper—with the word God on one and Heaven on the other, written as small as possible
▸ magnifying glass

aise your hand if you know the alphabet. Who can read? I have something in my bag that I want someone to try to read. Each of these pieces of paper has a word on it. Raise your hand if you think you can read this for me. *(God and Heaven.)* Was that easy to read? *(No.)* Why not? *(Too small.)* I have something else in my bag that helps people to read small print. (Show the children the magnifying glass.) Who can tell me what this is? It's called a "magnifying glass." It enlarges the item you are trying to see—it makes it bigger.

Let's see if it works. I'll hold it over the word on the paper, and you see if you can read it with the help of the magnifying glass. Did that help?

Did you know that God has "magnifiers" for each of you? He knows what is best for you, and He wants to help you make good decisions. So He has given you several gifts to help "magnify" your understanding as you grow to follow Him. Who can tell me what some of those gifts are? *(The Bible, Sabbath School, church, parents, teachers, pastors, and many more.)*

Each of these gifts can help you know what God wants for you as you grow up. You will have lots of decisions to make—who to choose as friends, what to study in school, what sport you want to learn for exercise, what foods are good for your body—many things to magnify and expand your lives.

All that Jesus wants is for you to take time to pray and to ask Him to lead you on the way. You will be busy learning and playing, but you will *never* be too busy for Jesus. Remember that all He wants is what is best for you. I hope you will begin and end every day by asking Him to lead your life as you grow up.

What You Need:
► one live plant

Something Alive

"That person is like a tree planted by streams of water,
which yields its fruit in season and whose leaf
does not wither—whatever they do prospers."

—Psalm 1:3, NIV

I have something in my bag that is alive. Would you like to see it? What is it? *(Plant.)* What does this plant need to keep it alive? *(Air, light, water, food, and soil.)* What happens if it stops getting any of these things? *(It dies.)* If I cut off a leaf, will the leaf die? What if I cut off a stem? Will it die? Yes, unless you can put it in water. Some plants can grow new roots when you put one of their stems in water. Some can't.

Did you know you have the ability to grow new roots? What would happen to you if you didn't drink any water or eat any food? *(You would die.)* But if you decided to start eating and drinking again, would you get well? *(Yes.)*

Your spiritual life with Jesus is the same! If you stop reading and praying, you will also stop growing to love Jesus, and you will die spiritually. Satan will tempt you to follow him instead and will make you think there is no such thing as sin. He lies to you. If you listen to him, he will teach you to sin. Sin is not OK. Sin takes us away from God. When you choose to sin, it will have the same result as when you stop eating and drinking. You will get weak, and Satan will continue to take you away from God.

Who can tell me what you should do to live for Jesus again? (Let the children respond.) What you have to do is pray and ask Jesus to come into your heart and to fill you with His love and kindness. When you are sorry for your sins and when you ask Jesus to forgive you, He will take away the sins.

Asking Jesus to forgive your sins is like growing new roots. You will get stronger and stronger. Every time Satan tries to tempt you to sin, you will ask Jesus to help you to say "No." And when Jesus comes, you will be ready to go with Him to heaven. Jesus has promised to give you eternal life, just for the asking! I hope you boys and girls will ask Jesus for new life every day.

Spark Plug

"John answered them all, 'I baptize you with water.
But one who is more powerful than I will come,
the straps of whose sandals I am not worthy to untie.
He will baptize you with the Holy Spirit and fire.' "
—Luke 3:16, NIV

I have something in my bag that is small but very powerful. I will show it to you; Does anyone know what it is? Do you need some clues? It is a part for a car. Now, can you guess? *(It is a spark plug.)*

Have you ever seen a spark plug in your family car? Some of the new cars have a big cover over the top of the motor, and you can't see the motor. Raise your hand if you think you know what a spark plug does for a car. It causes an electric spark that makes the gas inside your motor ignite, which then causes the motor to go around. If you give the motor more gas, it will make a bigger explosion in the motor and make the car go faster. If a spark plug stops working, the motor in your car will shake and make a bad noise, and your car will not run smoothly. If you don't repair it, you might damage the motor. Do you believe your car has spark plugs and that they are working, even though you can't see them? *(Yes.)* Yes, because your car is working smoothly, right?

The Holy Spirit is like a spark plug. You can't see Him, but you know He is an influence on you. The Holy Spirit is the One who speaks to your conscience to help you make a decision. He gives you a spark of life that wakes you up in the morning. He brings joy, happiness, peace, and strength to you. Has someone ever tried to get you to do something wrong? When that happened, was there something in your conscience that said, "Don't do that. It would be a wrong thing to do"? (Let the children respond.) That would be the Holy Spirit reminding you to say "No." When you are tempted to do wrong, the Holy Spirit will remind you that it would be a bad decision.

Now let's compare gasoline with our lives. Gas, the fuel that makes the spark plug power up, is like the time we spend in prayer and Bible study. If we have the spark but no gas, we can't go anywhere. Jesus has promised to supply us with the power we need to have full lives, but we have to follow His instructions.

I hope you will put "gas" in your life every day. What is the gas? Prayer and Bible study! Be sure to ask Jesus to put the spark in your life too! What is the Spark? The Holy Spirit! Jesus and the Holy Spirit will teach you to be a happy Christian. One day Jesus will come to take us all home to heaven. Raise your hand if you want to be with Jesus in heaven.

Stain Remover

" 'Come now, let us settle the matter,' says the LORD. 'Though your sins are like scarlet, they shall be as white as snow; though they are red as crimson, they shall be like wool.' " —Isaiah 1:18, NIV

"If we confess our sins, he is faithful and just and will forgive us our sins and purify us from all unrighteousness."
—1 John 1:9, NIV

There are six items in my bag that help us to keep things clean. Let's talk about each one separately. What does this one do? (Show each item, and let them children respond.)

Each of these items has something in common. What is it? (*All are used to clean.*) Some are used to keep *us* clean, and some are used on things that need cleaning. Can we wash our sins away with any of these cleaning products? (*No.*) How do we wash our sins away? First of all, we must be sorry that we sinned. Then we must tell Jesus that we are sorry and ask Him to forgive us. Jesus died for our sins, and the only way we can be forgiven is through Him. And when you ask, He will forgive.

Have you ever fallen down and gotten stains on your clothes when you were playing in the grass? Or have you ever spilled something on your clothes and gotten a stain that your parents were not able to remove? I have!

Let's see what the Bible says about Jesus taking our stains and sins away. (Read Isaiah 1:18.) When you have sinned, Satan comes around and whispers in your ear, "You are bad, and Jesus won't forgive you this time." Is this what is written in the Bible? (*No.*) (Read 1 John 1:9.) What do we need to do? Ask Jesus to forgive our sins.

Let's ask Jesus right now to take all our sins away, OK? (Pray.) "Dear Jesus, please take our sins away, and make us white as snow so we can live forever with You in heaven. Amen."

Take a Bath

"Create in me a pure heart, O God,
and renew a steadfast spirit within me."
—Psalm 51:10, NIV

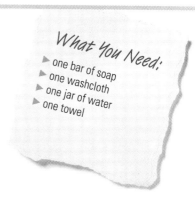

What You Need:
➤ one bar of soap
➤ one washcloth
➤ one jar of water
➤ one towel

Raise your hand if you have ever gotten muddy and dirty from playing outside. Was it fun? What did your parents tell you to do when you came back into the house? *(Take a bath!)* Your clothes were probably just as dirty as you. Did you take a bath with your clothes on? *(No.)* I did once! I was so dirty that my mother took me back outside and washed me all over with a hose—with my clothes on. Do you think I was clean after that? *(No.)* Do you think my clothes were clean? *(No.)* She just got the first layer off. I still had to go inside, take off my clothes, and get into the bathtub. Then my mom had to wash my clothes in the washing machine.

Can you get clean with just water? *(No.)* What else do you need? *(Soap.)* And sometimes bleach is needed to get stains out of the clothes. Do you think my little brother wanted to take a bath in my dirty water after I got clean? *(No.)* He wanted fresh water.

Let's compare the dirty bathwater with what is in our brains and in our hearts. Do you think our brains and hearts can get dirty? How can that happen? (Let the children respond.) There are programs on TV that have bad language, violence, and other things that are bad for you to see and hear. There are video games that have the same bad influence on you and will change how your brain thinks. Don't let Satan tempt you with these things. Don't let him tempt you to do or say mean things to your friends and family. Satan wants to dirty up your brain when he tempts you to do wrong.

Do you think we need "Jesus soap"? *(Yes.)* Jesus is the "soap" we need to clean away the sin in our lives. Instead of watching bad things on TV or playing bad games, let's find good games and concentrate on good things to say. Read your Bible, and don't forget to pray—and ask Jesus to help you think on good things.

How many of you want Jesus to be your "soap" and to clean your heart? Raise your hand if you want to go to heaven and live with Jesus. I do. Jesus wants to clean us on the inside and outside.

Teakettle

"A cheerful heart is good medicine,
but a crushed spirit dries up the bones."
—Proverbs 17:22, NIV

Raise your hands if you like to be happy. Are you happy right now? When you are happy, do you sit in the corner with a sad face? *(No.)* When we are happy, people can usually see it in our faces and in how we talk and act. Sometimes when we are *very* happy, we will giggle or laugh out loud. Isn't it fun to be happy?

I have something in my bag that lets you know when water starts boiling. Can you guess what it is? *(Teakettle.)* Have you ever seen one before? Teakettles are made in different shapes and sizes, just as you boys and girls are all different shapes and sizes. People don't use teakettles as often as they used to because there are many new ways to prepare hot drinks.

When water in a teakettle is put on a burner and heats up, it boils and starts to bubble. When that happens, steam rushes out of the spout, and you hear a whistle sound to let you know the water is boiling. I remember that when I was young, my mother would fill the teakettle with water as soon as she got up in the morning. She turned the stove on and put the kettle over the fire while she was getting our breakfast ready. I always knew it was time to get up when the teakettle started to whistle.

A whistling teakettle is a happy sound. Did you know Jesus wants us to be like the whistling teakettle when we wake up in the morning? He wants us to be happy as we begin our day. He will help us to be happy if we stop and have a few minutes of prayer time with Him before we get busy.

Jesus also likes for us to be happy Christians so that others will see Him living through us in the way we talk and act. That is a little like the steaming kettle singing its happy song. Remember to let Jesus' love bubble over in you.

Thankful List

"Always giving thanks to God the Father for everything,
in the name of our Lord Jesus Christ."
—Ephesians 5:20, NIV

Does anyone know the month that we celebrate Thanksgiving in? Do you think we should wait until Thanksgiving to think about things that we are thankful for? *(No.)*

I have a good idea for you, and I brought a sample of it in my bag for you to see. Shall I show it to you? Raise your hand if you can read what it says on the top of this paper. (Choose someone to read.) *(Thankful List.)* (Read some of the things on the list.) Would it be hard for you to make a thankful list? *(No.)* Who would like to tell me something that you are thankful for?

Have you ever told God how thankful you are for all the people and things He has blessed you with? Sometimes we get unhappy and complain if we don't have the new toy or the computer game we want. Do you get upset if you can't do something or go somewhere that you want to? Do you ever grumble because of such thoughts? The next time you feel unhappy about something, *stop* and take a minute to think about your thankful list. If you take time to think of that list, it will be harder for you to be unhappy.

If there is someone on your list whom you haven't told that you are thankful for, take time to let that person know. You can either write a note or give that person a call.

Can you think of Someone you should be *most* thankful to have in your life? *(Jesus.)* Yes, you can be most thankful for Jesus—thankful that He created you, that He forgives your sins when you ask, that He died on the cross to save you, and, most of all, that He is coming soon to take you to heaven. Raise your hand if you are thankful for all of those things. Don't forget to say "Thank You" to Jesus today.

What You Need:
- ► wax paper
- ► newspaper
- ► wrapping paper

Three Types of Paper

" 'For I know the plans I have for you,' declares the LORD,
'plans to prosper you and not to harm you,
plans to give you hope and a future.' "

—Jeremiah 29:11, NIV

I have three things in my bag that are all the same, but they each serve a different purpose. Each of them is a different size, but they are all flat. They are all made from a tree. Would you like to take a guess? This is a hard one, isn't it? So let's look at them, and you tell me how they are the same and why they are different. (Show the papers one by one, and let the children respond to what each is called.) *(Wax paper, newspaper, wrapping paper.)* How are they all the same? *(All are made from paper.)* Did you know that most paper is made from trees?

Now let's talk about how each of these papers needs to be different in order to be used for its special purpose. How would you like to read the newspaper if it was printed on this wax paper? Would you like to wrap a present in the wax paper? If you did that, you would be able to see what was inside, and it wouldn't be a surprise. How about wrapping your sandwich in newspaper? *(No.)* Each type of paper has a specific purpose.

Let's compare you boys and girls with how you are like paper. There are different types of paper, but they are still paper. You are the same in that you are all human beings and are all God's children. But each one of you is different, and God has a special job for you according to the talents He has given you. When you grow up, some of you will be teachers, doctors, nurses, firefighters, truck drivers, preachers, or one of many other jobs.

God has tasks for you even now, when you are young. Do you know what some of those tasks are? He wants you to be a friend to others, even to those whom no one else wants to be friends with. He wants you to be an example of Jesus; this means that while you are in school, in church, in Sabbath School, at home, or with friends, you will talk and act like Jesus talks and acts. You can find out how Jesus lives by reading in your Bible.

If you ask, Jesus will help you to live every day the way He wants you to live. When you wake up and get ready for your day, ask Jesus to be your guide all day long. If you do this every day, you will grow to be like Him. Raise your hand if you want to be like Jesus.

Three Trees and Three Seeds

What You Need:
▶ pinecone seeds
▶ acorn seeds
▶ sweet gum seeds

"The land produced vegetation: plants bearing seed according to their kinds and trees bearing fruit with seed in it according to their kinds. And God saw that it was good."
—Genesis 1:12, NIV

I have three things in my bag that can come alive! They all have the ability to make something tall or something short. They are all the same, but each has a different purpose. They are all different colors. Do you need more clues? Let me give you a big one. Sometimes these things have the ability to come alive and grow tall or short and are used to build houses. Now can you guess? *(Trees.)* Do you think I have three trees in my bag? *(No.)* Let me show you what I have! (Show the children the seeds.) Do these look like three trees? *(No.)* Do they look alive? *(No.)* What are they? *(Seeds!)* Is a seed a tree? *(No. Yes.)* If you said No or Yes, you are both right. The seeds are just trees that haven't grown yet. Can anyone guess what kind of a tree each seed came from? (Let the children respond.) *(Pine, oak, sweet gum.)*

I have some questions for you! Can an acorn grow into a pine tree? *(No.)* Can a pinecone grow into an oak tree? *(No.)* Can a sweet gum seed pod grow into a sweet gum tree? *(Yes.)* You are really smart. A seed can only grow into the kind of tree that the seed came from. Is what you see here the actual seed? *(No.)* Each one is the protective cover over the seed.

Let's compare you children to these three protective covers. You may look good on the outside, but it is what is inside that is important. You may grow up to be tall, short, strong, pretty, or handsome; but if you don't have Jesus inside you, you will not grow like Him. Tree seeds need nourishment for them to grow. You need the nourishment that only Jesus can give, in order for you to grow to be like Him.

Raise your hand if you want Jesus to protect you on the outside and to help you to grow like Him on the inside.

Time for Jesus

"In all your ways submit to him,
and he will make your paths straight."
—Proverbs 3:6, NIV

Raise your hand if you can tell me the two-letter word that you call yourself. *(Me.)* Very good! Let me show you "Me" (Bring out the "Me" jar.) Does this look like you or me? *(No.)* Let's just pretend the jar represents you or me as we start our day. It is empty, waiting to be filled with what you will do today. Since "Me" just got up, do you think it is a good idea to eat breakfast? *(Yes.)* Let's pour the "Eat Breakfast" bag of rice into the jar. After eating, would it be a good time to play for a while? Let's pour the "Play" bag of rice into the jar. Everyone needs a little fun! Maybe now it is time to rest and take a short nap. Does that sound good? *(No. Yes.)* Let's pour the "Sleep" bag of rice into the jar. What do you like to do after taking a nap? (Let the children respond.) How about watching TV? Be sure to choose carefully what you watch! Looks like you have had a busy day! The "Me" jar is pretty full!

Do you think "Me" should take time to study the Sabbath School lesson and pray? *(Yes.)* This is a good time to thank Jesus for His many blessings, especially for your parents. They are special. Let's put an egg into the jar. Now let's thank your angels for keeping you safe today. That, too, is very special, so let's add another egg to the jar. What about thanking Jesus for taking your sins away? That is a very special thank-You prayer. We'll add one more egg to the jar. Do you think it will fit? *(It won't fit!)* Hmm. I can't put the top on "Me" to close the day! Do you think we should leave Jesus out of our busy day? *(No.)* (Take the eggs out, and pour the rice back into one bag.)

Let me show you a better way! Let's put God in first. (Put the "God" egg in the jar.) Your prayer to Him is the most important anyway. We should have placed that prayer in right at first. Then eat. (Pour about one-third of the rice back into the jar.) During the day while you are playing and watching TV, stop to thank your angels for protecting you. (Put the "angels" egg in the jar, and pour another one-third of the rice in.) Before you go to sleep, take time to thank Jesus for taking your sins away. (Put the "Jesus" egg in and the remainder of the rice, then close the lid.)

If you follow this schedule, everything you need to do during the day will fit in perfectly. I hope you will remember to put God and Jesus first!

Toothbrush

What You Need:
▶ one toothbrush

"If we confess our sins, he is faithful and just and will forgive us
our sins and purify us from all unrighteousness."
—1 John 1:9, NIV

have something in my bag that comes in many colors, shapes, and sizes. It is
something your parents want you to use after you eat and before you go to bed
every day. It serves a very important purpose. Can you guess what it is? *(Tooth-brush.)* What does a toothbrush do? (Let the children respond.) *(Cleans teeth!)* Yes, and it
brushes away food and stains.

What might happen if you don't brush your teeth? (Let them respond.) *(Cavities.)*
Who can describe what a cavity is? (Let them respond.) *(A hole in your tooth.)* If you
have a hole in your tooth, pretty soon it will hurt a lot. If you don't get the cavity
fixed, you could lose your tooth. You might think that doesn't matter when you
are young because you will lose your baby teeth and get your permanent teeth; but
the cavity will still hurt, and it is still very important to take care of your teeth.

Can you think of anything that stains your life on the inside? When you have
done something wrong, what is that stain called? *(Sin.)* Sin can cause a "hurt"
inside of you.

Jesus has a different kind of "toothbrush" to deal with the problem of sin. Do
you know what it is? Prayer! You can ask Jesus to "brush" out the sin in your life.
If you don't ask Him to take your sins away, they can cause a huge hole in your
life, and you will feel a lot of pain.

Does Jesus promise to take your sins away? *(Yes.)* When you sin, you will feel
sorry in your heart; and when you tell Jesus you are sorry and ask Him to take the
sins away, He will. Satan is always trying to get you to do wrong. So you can also
ask Jesus to help remind you to say "No" every time Satan tempts you.

Jesus is coming from heaven to take us to live with Him there. There are streets
of gold and gates of pearls. They must be very shiny. Jesus wants to use His "tooth-brush" to forgive and brush away your sins, so you will be shiny on both the inside
and outside when He takes us to heaven.

What You Need:

▶ several toothpicks of different types and colors

Toothpicks

"Finally, brothers and sisters, whatever is true, whatever is noble, whatever is right, whatever is pure, whatever is lovely, whatever is admirable—if anything is excellent or praiseworthy—think about such things."

—Philippians 4:8, NIV

I have some things in my bag that are all alike but are all different. They all serve the same purpose, but some are longer than others. They can be round, square, or flat. They come in different colors. Some are plastic, and I've even seen some that are metal. Any guesses? (Let the children respond.) Most toothpicks are made from wood. Sometimes they have a point only on one end; but most of the time, they are pointed on both ends.

What are some of the things you can do with a toothpick? Have you ever played the game pick-up sticks? It is played by holding sticks that look like toothpicks, dropping them, and then trying to pick each one up without making any of the other sticks move. It is a fun game.

Let's compare a toothpick with a habit. It is easy to pick up a habit, either good or bad. A toothpick can be easily broken. If you hold several toothpicks together, it gets harder to break them. It is like a habit in that if you keep doing the same bad habit, it is harder to break.

Let me show you. Raise your hand if you would like to break this toothpick. (Choose someone.) Do you think you can break this toothpick? *(Yes.)* It is easy. OK, now let's try to break several at one time! It is much harder, isn't it? You might not be able to break them at all. Just like it is hard to break several toothpicks being held together, it is also hard to break bad habits. That is why we need to be careful what habits we pick up. We need to choose habits that are good for us.

Raise your hand if you can tell me what would be a good habit. (Let them respond.) *(Prayer, Bible study, kindness.)* Those are all good habits that we don't want to break, and we need to do them daily. If you have a bad habit that you want to break, you can pray and ask Jesus to help you to break that bad habit. Just like we were able to break the toothpick, Jesus is able to give you the strength to break a bad habit.

I want to give each of you a toothpick to keep on your dresser to help you remember to choose only good habits. Remember how hard it is to break a bad habit. Promise me you won't stick yourself or someone else with these, OK?

Two Buns

What You Need:
▶ two buns—one hamburger bun and one hot dog bun

"Then Jesus declared, 'I am the bread of life.
Whoever comes to me will never go hungry,
and whoever believes in me will never be thirsty.' "
—John 6:35, NIV

I have a trick question for you today. Are you ready? I have two different items that are the same in that they are both good to eat. They are brown, and you haven't eaten them. What are they? *(A hamburger bun and a hot dog bun.)* What is the trick part of the question? You haven't eaten them *yet!*

Is bread good for us? Some people think they have to eat bread every day. Do you think they had bread like this when Jesus lived here on the earth? *(No.)* It was probably different from these buns; while living on earth, Jesus did something important with bread. Can anyone think of a special story in the Bible that tells us something about bread? (Let the children respond.) Yes, Jesus fed five thousand people with five loaves and two fish. Bread is good for us, especially when blessed by Jesus.

Jesus told the people that He is "the Bread of Life" and that we will not be hungry if we follow Him. Let me read this to you from the Bible. (Read John 6:35.)

Do you think that if we follow Jesus every day, we won't have to eat or drink? *(No.)* That isn't what Jesus meant when He said those words. What He meant is that if we follow Him every day, we will live happy lives. We will do the things Jesus wants us to do, and He will keep us from sinning when we ask Him to. Jesus loves each of you very much and wants to take you to heaven.

What You Need:

► one raw egg
► one hard-boiled egg

Two Eggs

"Do not judge, and you will not be judged. Do not condemn, and you will not be condemned. Forgive, and you will be forgiven."

—Luke 6:37, NIV

I have two things in my bag. They look the same, but they are different. Let me give you some clues. They are hard on the outside and soft on the inside. They are not round but will roll. Would anyone like to take a guess? *(Eggs.)*

How are these two eggs the same? *(They are both white, the same size, and the same shape.)* So how are they different? (Let the children respond.) One is raw, and the other has been cooked. Can you tell me which egg has been boiled? *(No.)* The only way to know for sure is to crack the eggs open so that we can see the insides because we can't tell from the outside.

Sometimes you boys and girls can be compared to these two eggs. Would you like to know how? It is difficult to tell from the outside what you are thinking and whether you have good or bad thoughts. Only God can tell what you are thinking in your hearts and minds.

Sometimes we look at others, and we judge if they are good or bad by the way they dress or talk. It is true that if we hear them say bad words or see them being unkind to someone else, we should be careful about being friends with them. But sometimes we judge others without knowing enough about them, and we can't be sure about the kinds of people they are.

You should always ask Jesus to help you to be kind to everyone, even if they are different from you and say wrong things. Remember that only God can see our hearts. He wants all of you to love Him and to ask Him to help you be kind to *all* boys and girls.

Shall we see which egg is cooked? Let's check it out.

Two Ladies and One Glove

"When anxiety was great within me,
your consolation brought me joy."
—Psalm 94:19, NIV

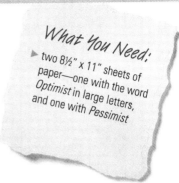

What You Need:
- two 8½" x 11" sheets of paper—one with the word *Optimist* in large letters, and one with *Pessimist*

My story today is about two words, two ladies, and one glove. Have any of you heard about a place called Atlanta, Georgia? On one very good day, the first lady in our story went into the city to help serve food to homeless and hungry people. There are homeless and hungry people everywhere, even here. These are people who don't have a place to live or money to buy food to eat. While this lady was working, she noticed another lady standing alone, wearing a thin coat. She had a cap on her head and only one glove for her hands. The lady was rubbing her hands together, trying to get warm. When the lady came through the line to get some food, the first lady said, "I see you lost your glove." She was very surprised when the lady told her, "No, I *found* a glove!" She smiled big at having found at least one glove to help her hand stay warm.

The two words I would like to teach you are *pessimist* and *optimist.* The pessimist looks at the lady and thinks, *Too bad; she has only one glove.* The optimist looks at the same lady and thinks, *How nice; she has found one glove to keep her hand warmer.* The pessimist will look at half a glass of water and think the glass is half-empty. The optimist will look at the same glass and think it is half-full. The pessimist keeps his (her) head down and sees all the trash that is on the ground, and the optimist looks up and sees the beautiful sky and stars at night.

Jesus wants us to be optimists, to always trust *Him* and keep looking up. We need to think positively, like the optimist, instead of negatively, like the pessimist. Even when you are unhappy or sick, remember that you can put your trust in Jesus and look on the positive side. He always wants the best for you, and He has a plan for your life. Ask Jesus to help you be an optimist and to look for the *best* in everything.

What You Need:
- two sheets of paper— with a bold straight line across one page, another with a wavy line across it
- one Bible

Two Lines in the Sand

"But if serving the Lord seems undesirable to you, then choose for yourselves this day whom you will serve, whether the gods your ancestors served beyond the Euphrates, or the gods of the Amorites, in whose land you are living. But as for me and my household, we will serve the Lord."

—Joshua 24:15, NIV

I have two sheets of paper in my bag illustrating something that I saw in the sand while walking on a beach. Would you like to see them? Can you guess what made the straight line in the sand? *(A bicycle.)* Raise your hand if you can ride a bicycle. It is fun, isn't it? Do you know how the crooked line was made? Also by a bicycle—but this bike was weaving back and forth in the sand. It looks like the bicycle that made the crooked line didn't follow the leader who made the straight line. If the leader goes to the right or left, sometimes the follower will follow the same path, right?

How do you think these lines are like our lives? Each of you (we grown-ups too) has to make decisions every day whether to follow Jesus (the straight line) or to follow Satan (the cooked line). Those are the only two choices, Jesus or Satan. If we choose to follow Satan, he will tempt us to do things that are wrong and try to make us think we can still go to heaven. Remember the story about how he tricked Eve in the Garden of Eden by telling her not to listen to God when He said not to eat the fruit from that tree. Satan lied and told her it was OK to eat it. Did the devil tell the truth? *(No.)* Satan cannot be trusted to tell the truth. He lied to Eve, and he will lie to you.

Jesus is the straight line! It can be more difficult to ride in a straight line; but if we ask Jesus to help us, we can do it. Joshua 24:15 states, "Choose you this day whom ye will serve" (KJV). If your life is a little crooked, ask Jesus to help you go in a straight line. Choose to follow Jesus to heaven.

Hermit Crab Shells

What You Need:
▶ two hermit crab shells—one polished and one rough

"In the same way, let your light shine before others, that they may see your good deeds and glorify your Father in heaven."
—Matthew 5:16, NIV

I have two things in my bag that are the same but look very different. Both were alive at one time but are now dead. Need another clue? They lived in the ocean at one time. *(Shells.)* (Show the children.) Do they look the same? *(No, why not?)* One is dull and rough, and the other is shiny. Do you know how this one got shiny? Someone polished it. The person rubbed off all the rough coating that had grown on the outside of the shell. Isn't the shell beautiful when it is polished?

Let's see if we can compare the shells to you boys and girls. While you are growing up, Satan is always trying to get you to do and say things that lead you away from Jesus. Satan wants you to look like this shell with the rough coating. It looks bad. He wants you to make wrong choices. If you choose to speak nicely, do kind things, and talk sweetly to your mom and dad, Satan will have to walk away because you have listened to the Holy Spirit instead and have made a better choice than what Satan was suggesting. Unfortunately, that doesn't mean he will give up; Satan doesn't give up easily, and he will be back again to tempt you.

If you pray and ask Jesus to polish your life, it will shine like the beautiful shell. He is more than willing and able to help you every day. When Jesus forgives and takes away your sins, you will shine for Him, just like this shell shines.

Raise your hand if you want Jesus to shine you up. How often should you pray this prayer? Every day!

What You Need:
- two straws
- one pint of water
- two straws for each child

Two Straws

"And let the one who wishes take
the free gift of the water of life."
—Revelation 22:17, NIV

Would you like to see what I have in my bag today? Before I show you, I will give you a clue to see if you can guess what I have. Sometimes you boys and girls like to use this to blow bubbles. Sometimes when you are sick and lying in bed, it helps for you to use it to take a drink. Who can guess what it is? *(Straw.)* Do you like to drink with a straw? Is it easier to drink with a straw? *(Yes.)*

I need a helper. (Choose an older child.) I have a jar of water, and I want to see if you can drink some of it with this straw. Was that easy? *(Yes.)* If I give you another straw so that you will have two instead of one, do you think it will be easier? *(Yes.)* (Put one straw in the water and one outside the jar. Let the child try.) Is it easy now? *(No.)* Do you know why it is harder? The one straw is trying to pick up the water, which is heavy, and the other is picking up the air, which is lighter.

Did you know that following Jesus is a little like trying to drink water with a straw? When you decide you want to do what Jesus says, it is like drinking with one straw. It isn't hard. However, if you decide to follow Jesus sometimes and Satan sometimes, it will be like trying to use two straws—with one in the water and one on the outside of the jar. In the Bible, Jesus is referred to as having the "water of life," and He invites you to draw (drink from His straw) that water from Him. Satan doesn't want you to make that decision. He offers you another "straw"—his way—and that makes life difficult.

How many straws do you want to use to help you get to heaven? *(One.)* The one that Jesus offers is the easier one to use. I brought two straws for each of you so that you can try this test yourself. You can keep them in your room to remind you to drink only from the straw that Jesus offers, and that will make your life better.

Valentine's Day

What You Need:
➤ one picture of a heart on a sheet of paper

"My son, give me your heart and
let your eyes delight in my ways."
—Proverbs 23:26, NIV

I have a question for you today. Raise your hand if you know what holiday comes around in February, February 14 to be exact. Does anyone know? *(Valentine's Day.)* What is special about this day?

On Valentine's Day, people like to give and receive greeting cards, boxes of candy, or bouquets of flowers to show their love to the people they care about. Is there a special sign that reminds you of this day? *(A heart.)* Is it fun to make a card for your mom and dad to let them know you love them, or one for your best friend? The heart sign is used because love comes from your heart.

When you go home today, why not draw a heart sign and write a note or draw a picture on it and give it to your mom and dad to let them know how much you love them?

Would you like to give a love gift to your best Friend, Jesus? Your heart is the best gift you can give to Him. That means that you love Jesus with all of your heart. And do you think Jesus loves you? Let's sing "Jesus Loves Me" as a reminder of how much He loves you.

Vegetable Soup and the Christian

"Jesus answered, 'I am the way and the truth and the life. No one comes to the Father except through me.' "

—John 14:6, NIV

want to make two different things for you to see today. Do you want to see what I have in my bag? Let me show you. (Show the children the pan, the water, the potatoes, and the carrots.) Can you tell me what I will be making? *(Soup.)* Would you like a taste of my soup? *(No, it's not soup.)* Not soup? I have the right ingredients for it to be soup. What is wrong? *(Have to cook it.)*

Well, let me assemble the second thing that I want to make for you. OK, I'll get my Sabbath School lesson, my devotional book, my Bible, and my offering envelope. It looks like I've made a Christian. I have all of the ingredients. What do you think? Have I made a Christian? *(No.)* You are right. Just because I have all of the things I need to be a Christian that doesn't make me a Christian. So what do I need? I need to pray for Jesus to take control of my life. He gives me these tools, these things I have gathered, to help me along the way, but what He really wants first is for me to give my heart to Him and to love Him.

So remember that Jesus has given you all of the tools you need to become a Christian, which means you want to become like Him (Christlike), but the most important thing that He wants is for you to give Him your heart. Let's pray and ask Jesus for His help.

Warning Labels

What You Need:
- boxes
- bottles with warning labels
- one Bible

"So, as the Holy Spirit says: 'Today, if you hear his voice, do not harden your hearts as you did in the rebellion, during the time of testing in the wilderness.' "
—Hebrews 3:7, 8, NIV

I have several things in my bag that many of you probably have in your homes. Because I think it might be hard for you to guess, I will just show these things to you. Would you like to see them? These are things that have words written on them that are very important for you to learn about. Here are some of the words: *warning, danger, caution,* and *poison.* Why do you think these warnings need to be written on the bottles, cans, and boxes? Because the contents on the inside could make you very sick, sick enough to die. And if you didn't know that ahead of time, you might eat or drink one of them, thinking it wouldn't hurt you.

Did you know that Jesus has given us words of warning? Do you know where to look for them? *(The Bible.)* Jesus wants you to hear or read the Bible warnings so that you will learn what they are and will not get spiritually sick. An example is in Hebrews 3:7. In my Bible, it says, "Warning." Let me read it to you: "Oh, that today you would listen as he speaks" (NET). That means that when you hear or read these words, God is speaking to *you*, and you should listen to and follow the advice He is giving you. Satan says, "Do not listen to God." He doesn't want you to pay attention to God's warnings. Don't listen to Satan's bad advice.

I hope you will always watch out for warning signs to keep you from getting sick. Also look for the warnings found in the Bible. When you pay attention to God's warnings, you will be saved from a lot of trouble. Remember that the reason Jesus gives you these warnings is that He loves you and wants you to be with Him in heaven.

Watch

"Better the poor whose walk is blameless than the rich whose ways are perverse."
—Proverbs 28:6, NIV

The item I have in my bag is something that will not say anything but will tell you something! Does that sound confusing? This item sometimes has a round shape and sometimes a square shape. Would you like to take a guess? It can tell you the time, the date, and some other things. Now do you know? *(A watch.)*

How can a watch tell you something without talking? Well, it really doesn't "tell" you. It is something you can read on it. There are some watches now that will talk to you, but this isn't one of them.

Let's compare you boys and girls with a watch. How can that be? Sometimes you give people a message about the kind of person you are by the way you speak, act, or dress. They will "read" what you are like by the way you treat your parents, your friends, your teachers, and strangers. They can tell if you represent Jesus and if He is in your heart. I don't have to tell you who you represent if Jesus is not your helper. Satan wants you to make choices that represent him, and those are choices you need to stay away from.

Raise your hand if you want to go with Jesus when He comes to take us to heaven. I hope you will choose Jesus so that when people "read" you, you will tell them by the way you live that you belong to Him. Let's pray and ask Him to help.

Water

"Whatever your hand finds to do, do it with all your might, for in the realm of the dead, where you are going, there is neither working nor planning nor knowledge nor wisdom."
—Ecclesiastes 9:10, NIV

Let's see if you can guess what I have in my bag today. I have a jar of something you use every day. It is always wet, never dry! Can you guess what it is? Need another clue? It is clear, but you can make it colored. You cannot live without it. Now do you know? *(Water.)* (Show jar of water.)

What happens when cold water reaches 32 degrees Fahrenheit? It freezes! What good things can we do with frozen water or ice? *(Put in drinks, ice-skate, put on a swollen arm or leg.)* What can you do with hot water? *(You can cook, take a hot bath, and put your hands and feet in it when you are cold.)* What happens when water reaches 212 degrees? *(It makes steam, and it boils away.)*

Did you know there are some ways your heart and mind can be compared to water? When you get cold, your heart slows down, and when you are hot, it speeds up. If you stop reading your Bible and stop praying to Jesus, your heart will slowly grow cold, like water turns to ice, and you will no longer be happy. If you fill your heart and mind with knowing Jesus better, He will fill you with happiness and joy. You will be like the boiling water making steam. Everyone will be able to see that you have Jesus in your mind and heart.

How do you feel about knowing Jesus today? Are you boiling over with the happiness of having Jesus in your life, or do you act like you do not know Jesus? I hope each of you will take time to read your Bible or to have your parents read it to you. Take time to pray to Jesus every day and ask Him to fill you with His love and happiness.

What You Need:

▶ three CDs or DVDs—the first one with the right cover on the CD or DVD, the second with an incorrect CD or DVD; the third missing the CD or DVD inside the cover

What Is on the Inside?

"In the same way, on the outside you appear to people as righteous but on the inside you are full of hypocrisy and wickedness."

—Matthew 23:28, NIV

I have three things in my bag that are all the same but are all different. Shall I give you some hints? They all hold something inside of them. They can be used in your home or in your car—something that you would look at or listen to. Hold up your hand if you think you can guess what I have. *(DVDs, CDs.)*

Let's take a look and see what these three covers have in them. OK, what is inside this first one? Let's read the title on the cover. What does it say? (Let someone respond.) OK, let's look inside to see if you are right. What is the title on the CD (DVD)? You should be able to tell what is on the inside based on what is on the outside. Is that correct? *(Yes. No.)* So is the title on the CD (DVD) the same as the one on the cover? Yes, it is.

OK, let's look at number two. (Choose someone to read the cover.) What does it say on this cover? Let's see what is inside. What is the title on the disc? Is it the same? *(No!)* I guess you can't always tell what is on the inside based on what is on the outside! So let's look at the third one. What does this cover say? OK, let's look inside. There isn't a disc in this one! Wow! When you look on the outside, you can't tell if there is something on the inside, can you?

I guess we really need to check closely to be sure that what is on the inside matches what is on the outside. Now let's compare you boy and girls with these CD (DVD) covers. If the way you talk and act represents Jesus, you can trust that what is on the outside will be like what is on the inside. That would be like our number one example, right?

If you look good on the outside but are not like Jesus on the inside, you don't match up, just like our number two example had a different CD (DVD) on the inside than what the cover said on the outside. Sometimes kids act like they are your friends; but if they act as if they don't even know you at other times, then that is not true friendship. Be careful, though, not to judge other children based on what you see on the outside. Only God knows what is in someone's heart. Ask Jesus to help you choose wisely when it comes to making friends. He will guide you to choose carefully. Let's pray that you will choose to be the same both inside and outside.

White Thread

"I can do all this through him
who gives me strength."
—Philippians 4:13, NIV

What You Need:
► one spool of white thread
► one pair of scissors

oday I have something in my bag that is small and round and has something wrapped around it. It is available in many colors and is used to hold or connect things together. You may have several of these in a basket at home. Raise your hand if you think you know what it is. Need another clue? Whoever made your clothes would need this item to make the cloth hold together. (Show spool of thread.)

Let's pretend this white thread is a sin. I need a volunteer! (Choose someone who is strong.) Hold the end of this thread very tightly, and keep your hands down at your side. Don't let go of the thread.

Can you tell me what might be a sin, beside lying? (Let the children respond, and choose one of their suggestions to talk about. As you start talking about the subject, walk around the child while wrapping him or her up with the thread. Go around three to four times.)

Is it easy to sin the first time? It is not easy to sin when your conscience tells you not to. But the more you sin, the less you think about it. The less you think about it, the more it can become a habit. Now raise your arms and break the thread. (Be sure the child does not let go of the end.) You can see it is easy to break the thread. (After the thread breaks, say the following.) Just as the string broke easily, bad habits are easy to break when you ask Jesus to take control and to help you change. Now I want you to do the same thing again. Put your arm down, and hold on to the string tightly. (Wrap the thread around the child *many times*. You will have to test this before doing it.)

If you let Satan tempt you to do wrong and you keep giving in to him, he will gradually influence you to do more and more wrong things. Your moms and dads want to help you to stay away from Satan and want to help you to avoid bad habits. (Stop and see if the child can break the thread.) Looks like this bad habit has become very *hard* to break! But when you are willing to let Jesus help, He is right there to do away with the bad habit. (Take the scissors, and cut the thread.) All you have to do is ask Jesus for forgiveness, and He will free you. Jesus will protect you as long as you pray and listen to Him.

Remember Philippians 4:13: "I can do all things through Christ who strengthens me" (NKJV).

White Washcloth

"If we confess our sins, he is faithful and just and will forgive us our sins and purify us from all unrighteousness."

—1 John 1:9, NIV

I have something in my bag that helps keep us clean. You probably use one on your face in the morning when you get up. Can you guess what it is? *(A washcloth.)* This is a special washcloth because it is white. I will explain why in a minute. How does a washcloth help us get clean? When you wet the washcloth and rub it on your skin, the dirt from your skin is transferred to the washcloth. When you wash your dirty hands, do you ever look at the washcloth to see how dirty it gets? Your parents have to wash the cloth to get it clean again.

Now I want to tell you why this white washcloth is special. Do you know who takes away our sins and cleans the dirt out of our minds and hearts? *(Jesus.)* He took our sins on Himself and then died on the cross to wash them all away. He makes you white, just like this washcloth. He does not have to die again. When God the Father looks at us, He looks at Jesus, who has no sin.

Do you want to have Jesus wash your sins away so that you will be clean, just like this white washcloth? I hope that when you take a bath and wash your hands or face, you will remember to stop and thank Jesus for forgiving you and taking your sins away. Let's ask Jesus to wash our sins away now!